REACHING THE CHASM

HOW TO
DRIVE YOUR
EARLY-STAGE START-UP
TO SCALE

REACHING
THE
CHASM

EDWARD G. AMOROSO

Columbia Business School
Publishing

Columbia University Press
Publishers Since 1893
New York   Chichester, West Sussex
cup.columbia.edu

Library of Congress Cataloging-in-Publication Data
Names: Amoroso, Edward G. author
Title: Reaching the chasm : how to drive your early-stage start-up to scale /
Edward G. Amoroso.
Description: New York : Columbia University Press, [2025] | Includes index.
Identifiers: LCCN 2025015353 | ISBN 9780231219839 hardback |
ISBN 9780231562928 ebook
Subjects: LCSH: New business enterprises—United States |
Entrepreneurship—United States |
Technological innovations—United States
Classification: LCC HD62.5 .A487 2025 | DDC 658.1/10973—
dc23/eng/20250718
LC record available at https://lccn.loc.gov/2025015353

Cover design: Noah Arlow
Cover image: Shutterstock

GPSR Authorized Representative: Easy Access System Europe,
Mustamäe tee 50, 10621 Tallinn, Estonia, gpsr.requests@easproject.com

CONTENTS

CONTENTS

PART FOUR Review and Planning

PREFACE

Start-Ups Are Harder Than They Look. *Much Harder.*

During the past decade, my workday has started early in the morning with reviews of start-ups. It continues throughout the day with reviews of more start-ups. And it closes well into the evening with more time spent with start-ups. I use Zoom, GoTo Meeting, Webex, and Teams. And I'll occasionally hold old-fashioned, face-to-face business meetings in the Manhattan offices of TAG Infosphere Inc. (yes, it's a start-up), where I serve as the company's founder and CEO.

I believe that during these past few years, I've spent as much time reviewing and working with start-ups as any other human being. I do this because it is my passion—and I believe that I've been helpful to the bold entrepreneurs launching these new companies. Most of them are trying to get their airplane off the ground, so to speak—and that's been my sweet spot: start-ups in the early stage trying to get their first customers.

Some founders have had to be peeled off the ceiling after I've been, well, *direct* with my feedback. I've had colleagues tell me after a particularly lively session that I might have insulted the founder. And yes, I probably did. But so be it. Call it tough love. Call it whatever, but I've tried to be an honest broker with founders who've invested so much of their time and effort trying to make their businesses grow.

They deserve the truth—and so do you.

TAG focuses mostly on cybersecurity start-ups in business-to-business (B2B) settings, but we've recently extended our work to artificial intelligence, sustainability, cloud computing, financial technology, and more. We are also now working with business-to-consumer (B2C) companies. You should find the advice here useful regardless of your industry, but we warn you that this is written for early-stage companies. If you have billions in revenue, then this is not for you.

I would be remiss not to mention the world-class team of advisers and analysts we employ at TAG. Nothing I describe here would have been possible without their assistance. You should also know that TAG is *not* an investment group, which is unusual because most teams reviewing start-ups are interested in equity. That is not us. We do collect advisory fees, but we try to remain unbiased when providing guidance—and I'll stick to that approach in this book.

Such a purpose-driven approach should help to illustrate why thousands of start-ups have been willing to tell us their story. They understand that influencing TAG, like all analyst firms, is a necessary business marketing step. And our work with start-ups is often demanded by their investors. But we believe that our clients view us as a friend, not a foe, and that *our* mission is to help them identify *their* mission (more on this below).

Reviewing and advising founding teams is especially tough when the principals refuse to acknowledge the following fact: *Start-ups are much harder to run than entrepreneurs think.* And it doesn't help that many new companies are managed by young and aggressive folks who have a wonderful dream and passion but often little experience operating an actual business. This is not easy stuff, so founders should strap in for a turbulent ride.

The entrepreneurs we work with come from all walks of life. They include the Israeli defense graduate starting a security firm, the physics major trying to make fusion work, the bored accountant quitting the Big Firm to create a new cloud-based tax-reporting app. And yes, they also include the inevitable programmer nerds trying to become the next Facebook. The common denominator is enthusiasm, but as I will show in this book, enthusiasm is not enough.

Start-ups exist in many different stages of development. Some are in stealth, trying to build a minimum viable product (MVP) (whatever *that* means). Others begin as service companies like TAG, collecting fees to self-fund a product that can generate annual recurring revenue (ARR), which is viewed by many start-ups as their Holy Grail. And still others are swelled with seed money or series A dollars that make them feel like masters of the universe.

Our focus here is on start-ups trying to build to the famous gap identified years ago by management consultant Geoffrey Moore. His book, *Crossing the Chasm*, literally defined the initial base camp for early-stage start-ups—namely, the *chasm*. The chasm refers to an inevitable pause in the growth journey where a start-up must shift from early buyers to a mass market. Our purpose is *not* to help you cross the chasm but rather to help you *reach* the chasm.

As shown in figure 0.1, the stages of Geoffrey Moore's now-iconic business model involve five distinct periods of growth for any new

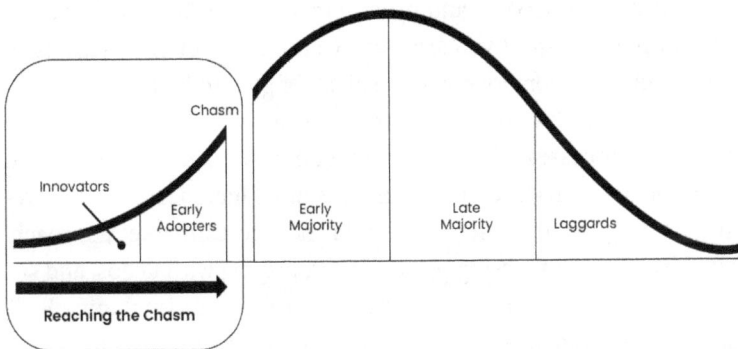

Figure 0.1 Reaching the Chasm

company. The first two stages involve selling a new product or service to innovators and early adopters. Both buyer types are likely to enjoy disruption and are typically willing to take risk with an early-stage start-up to reap potential benefits. Traversing these stages is what we refer to as reaching the chasm.

In Moore's model, the chasm is a gulf that must be navigated to shift the early-stage start-up toward a new approach that can scale to a mass market. His amazing book has helped millions of companies find a way to reinvent themselves to support scale. Few books have had as much impact on the business community, and our own team at TAG is currently navigating our own chasm to scaled growth, which isn't easy.

You can think of this book as a guided tour for early-stage start-ups trying to reach the chasm. Yes, much of our guidance will also apply to larger start-ups who are scaling to growth, perhaps with series C, series D, or even initial public offering (IPO) funding. But our primary focus is on the entrepreneurs who are working eighty-hour weeks doing whatever is necessary to get that first bank, first telecom, or first retail firm to take a chance on their product.

Here's one important aspect of the early-stage challenge: While mature B2B companies are usually staffed to handle the day-to-day needs of supporting customers, early-stage start-ups must develop sufficient maturity to understand legal contracting, risk management, customer service, and procurement. Older founders have an advantage here—so if you are just five minutes out of college, then you should find someone with a splash of gray to help.

By the way, B2C start-ups can get away with less focus on the business processes of buyers. But contrary to every Hollywood script on start-ups, even B2C start-ups must include a dose of careful planning and dead seriousness in their go-to-market approach. The idea of coders tossing paper planes, playing with Legos, and sitting around gaming is a silly fantasy. Every start-up, including B2C, demands a willingness to accept *gut-wrenching* hard work.

As suggested above, mature company leaders might benefit to some degree from this book, but probably not so directly. Once a start-up grows into a large company, perhaps trading on a public exchange, things shift considerably. I worked for decades as a senior executive at AT&T—and its inner workings are *completely different* than a start-up. The incentives, processes, structures, and regulations are just plain different because they have to be.

I've also seen these differences from a governance perspective, having served on the board of directors at M&T Bank, an institution that did not and should not resemble a start-up. Thus, the advice and guidance offered in the following chapters are written primarily for early-stage start-up companies trying to reach the chasm. Please keep that in mind as you flip through the pages of this book. I am aiming the arrow at early-stage capitalists.

Founders almost always miss the fact that the features in their MVP will *not* be the reason they attract early buyers. Start-ups struggle with this idea because most popular business guidance assumes a rational buying process. But when you are a start-up, you must accept the irrationality of anyone other than your parents writing you a check. The likelihood of your continued existence is low, and your competitors will usually have better products. Those are just facts.

What you bring to the table is that you are *new*. This is why we always—and I mean, *always*—explain to start-ups that their *belief system* will be one hundred times more powerful in attracting new buyers than the functionality of their product. I will spend a great deal of time on this point in the first part of this book, and readers would be wise to read slowly through the early chapters.

Let me repeat this: The secret key to reaching the chasm, if there is one, involves belief systems. Write that down.

I hope that you will also learn that when early sales are not meeting expectations, the day-to-day mechanics of running a start-up are usually not the problem. Inexpensive SaaS solutions exist to support accounting, payroll, project management, and customer relationship management. We have found that start-ups are usually adept with these online tools. In fact, they are sometimes *too* adept at the tools, and it diverts their focus (more on this below).

The reality is that, when a start-up is not making its numbers, the main problem rarely involves the type of explanations offered in business school. If you are having trouble with early sales, then I can assure you with the highest degree of confidence that the problem is not insufficient funding, high interest rates, slow economic growth, or geopolitics. The problem is more visceral, and it involves something called a *purpose for being*.

Let me repeat this: If your early-stage start-up is not making its numbers, then it is almost never because you do not have the right features in your MVP. Instead, the reason you are not making your numbers will exist more in the collective thoughts and attitudes of the founding team than in the features and capabilities of the offer. Buyers of early-stage products buy into your purpose and mission—and if you do not have both, then you will not reach the chasm.

Chapter 1 is the most important chapter in the book. If, after reading the advice in it, your view of your own start-up has not been transformed, then please just toss this book into the recycle bin.

Now, go ahead and turn the page, and let's get started.

PART ONE

DISCOVERY AND LEARNING

1

WHY ARE YOU IN BUSINESS?

I will assume that you are either running an early-stage start-up, considering running a start-up, or have a close relationship to a start-up. Perhaps you are an investor in a start-up, or an employee in a start-up, or perhaps the spouse of someone running a start-up (my condolences). And when we reference *start-up*, we mean that you are not yet in the process of scaling to a massive crowd of customers. You are still working to build an initial customer base.

We can further assume that when we talk about *your start-up*, this reference has some practical and financial meaning to you. You have either quit a job, borrowed from family members, or taken some other seemingly irrational step to chase your dream. And failure would have real consequences not just on your checking account balance but also on your psyche. I will thus assume that you have taken the plunge and that you are emotionally *invested*.

Let's also make believe that you've set up time with me for advisory guidance and that we are now engaged in our initial discussion about your start-up. Maybe your venture capital team has urged you to speak with me because this is a common use-case for our work. We've dispensed with the silly pre-Zoom-call pleasantries about the weather in Tel Aviv or Palo Alto—and now it is time to get down to brass tacks. I will begin the session with this simple request:

Tell me about your start-up.

I make this simple request of start-up founders with every possible demographic profile imaginable. They could be experienced leaders trying a start-up, repeat founders trying to duplicate a prior exit, young first-time founders just out of Stanford or New York University (NYU), or corporate misfits who are trying something new. The point is that I will always start by making this basic request regardless of the situation: *Tell me about your start-up.*

Take a moment to think about how you would respond. You can assume that I am reasonably knowledgeable about your area but perhaps not an expert. So what would you say? I'll pause here as you think. (I'll hum the *Jeopardy* theme.)

My experience has been that the vast majority of founders and founding teams tell me *what they do* when they are asked to share information about their start-up. They might say this: "We provide an advanced approach to AI-based data analysis." Or: "We offer a cloud-based platform that secures the Internet of Things for hospitals." Or: "We provide organic composting solutions for industrial facilities."

It is an amazingly uniform response. Founders tell us *what* they do. "We do this. We do that." We hear this response so often that we suspect that founders have all read the same book about how to describe their company. And we have watched venture capital teams and other stakeholders reinforce this approach: *Describe what you do*, they will coach their portfolio companies. *Explain your solution clearly.*

What was *your* response to my simple inquiry? I'll bet it involved explaining what you do. Assuming I am right, then we are ready to begin reprogramming you to claw your way to that chasm. The goal is to shift your mindset from *what you do* to one that focuses on something much more powerful. We believe that the secret to building an initial customer base in an early-stage start-up demands that you focus on *why*.

THE POWER OF SIMON SINEK'S "WHY"

I generally allow founders a few minutes to tell me *what they do* before I will interrupt and remind them that I did *not* ask them to explain the functionality of their product or service. I did not ask them to define the problem that their carefully conceived solution was designed to address. Rather—and I always point this out explicitly—I just asked them to tell me about their business. It's a simple request, begging a simple answer.

So I usually repeat the request—*Tell me about your business.* I invariably get the same response about products, features, and capabilities, albeit with different words. The second response usually involves more words. It always amazes me that founders are rarely succinct in their description of anything, much less what their business is all about. They seem to like talking, and this is unfortunate because they should be listening, not talking.

Sometimes, I'll play back verbatim the founder's description of their start-up, often to that person's legitimate horror. This is a helpful practice, by the way—one I highly recommend. Have someone ask you about your company. Have them play back what you said and see if you too are falling into the trap of talking too much. It's not a good look for a start-up founder. Fewer words are the key.

We will eventually discuss the difference between *what* a company does and the more visceral issue of *how* and *why* the company does what it does. And yes, there is also a difference between *how* and *why*. Our observation, as shown below, is that no one has ever explained these differences better than the famous Simon Sinek. In fact, his work is so relevant that we will take some time here to review his most salient points.

In his best-selling book, *Start with Why*, Simon Sinek points out with great force and clarity this issue that we see every day in our work at TAG with start-ups. Through his narrative and examples, which we interpret in the context of start-ups, Sinek shows that it is much more powerful to explain one's early-stage business in the context of why it was started than to provide details on what it does. And yes, this might seem awkward, but bear with me.

With his now famous Golden Circle diagrams, immortalized in a TED talk seen by millions (although many founders we talk with have barely heard of the book or author), Sinek lays out his views in a highly convincing manner. His basic premise is that buyers will purchase products from people who "believe what you believe." He explains that companies, when sharing their narrative, should start with the innermost circle in figure 1.1 and then move outward.

As shown in figure 1.1, the innermost circle of the Golden Circle model is labeled "why," the next surrounding circle is labeled "how," and the outermost circle is labeled "what." Sinek expertly explains that the weakest way to describe a company starts with "what" and moves inward in the model. Too many companies, he explains, start with a description of what they do, and then get around (or don't get around) to explaining the motivation and belief system driving such approach.

Instead, Sinek argues that the correct response to the request *Tell me about your company* should begin with why it exists in the first

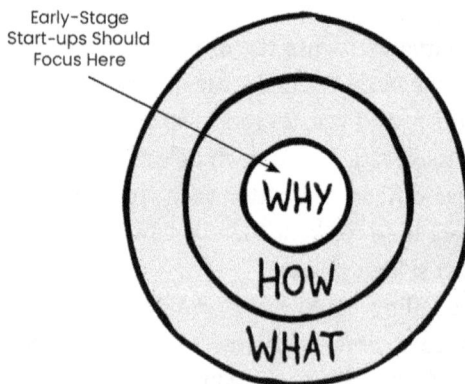

Figure 1.1 Simon Sinek's Golden Circle

place, and we believe the advice is perfect for start-up founders. The belief system driving your start-up will differentiate you from more powerful competitors because it is unique to you. If I believe what you believe, then I am apt to consider buying from you.

In his talks, books, and appearances, Sinek uses examples such as Martin Luther King Jr., whose product was a powerful idea about how our society should work. Sinek points out that King said, "I believe," in his great speech in Washington, and that he repeated one key phrase: "I have a dream." Imagine, Sinek explains, if King had said: "I have a plan." It's obvious that this would have had less impact.

THE INSPIRING EXAMPLE OF APPLE'S "WHY"

I've had the privilege to have worked closely with Apple over the years. While at AT&T, I was in charge of network security during many iPhone launches, and as part of these efforts, I was exposed to Apple's corporate approach. I'd also been assigned to Apple as their AT&T corporate executive (ACE) representative, which meant that I was the seniormost executive who Apple could contact for any reason that would benefit from stepping outside normal channels.

During this time, I became friendly with Gil Amelio, Apple's CEO at the time, perhaps best known as the executive who later brought Steve Jobs back to Apple. He was also a member of the AT&T board of directors at the time. I mention these connections because I've had the ability to interact on a personal level with people at Apple for many years. My knowledge of the company has been firsthand as opposed to just reading about them in books.

During my time interacting with that company, I personally saw that many different executives, staff members, software developers, and other members of Apple's company were asked to talk about their employer—and in fact to address the inquiry: *Tell me about your company.* I can tell you that I never once heard an employee say that "Apple makes iPhones," or "Apple develops software," or any other statement of *what* the company does.

Yes, they eventually get around to this in the conversation because, of course, you have to explain what you do. And I am not suggesting that members of any start-up or vendor (and, remember, Apple is not a start-up) not focus on their products. But I am suggesting that your first instinct when asked about your company should be to talk about why the company exists versus what the company does.

For Apple, employees' responses to the request have always been some version of "We think differently," or "We challenge the status quo." This is repeated so much that when one says these statements out of any context, listeners immediately connect the references with Apple. It's exactly the right approach, and it is part of the key to developing a visceral relationship with early adopters. And that secret key is this:

> Early buyers will make purchase decisions *based on your purpose* rather than your product. Take a moment to absorb this point because it offers essential insight into how you drive success in an early-stage start-up.

I was browsing through the iconic Philip Williams Poster Museum in New York City several years ago when I happened to find an original *Think Different* poster from Apple in the late 1980s. It showed the famous picture of Buzz Aldrin taken by Neil Armstrong and that old retro Apple logo is on top next to the statement: *Think Different.* That is an amazing purpose statement.

I bought the poster, and a framed copy of this amazing message has hung behind the desk in my home office ever since. If you watch any YouTube videos of me interviewing security executives as part of our TAG series, you will see it on the wall behind me. That poster reminds me every day, as I run my own start-up and as I review the approach being taken by other start-up founders, always to start with *why* you are in business.

Another point is that, whenever I bring up Apple in advisory sessions with new companies, eventually someone starts rolling their eyes and suggesting that I am comparing apples and oranges (and they'll often excuse the pun). They'll remind me that Apple is a multitrillion-dollar company, so, of course, they can have a broad belief system. They are like a small country. "Why," they ask, "would you compare our little company to such a massive giant?"

I always answer by reminding them that, like their own start-up, Apple was once a tiny company. And I can assure you that Steve Jobs and Steve Wozniak were on a stated mission with a clear purpose. Go back and read their comments during the early days in the 1970s. It was never about making computers. It was always about changing the world—often by taking on and slaying the IBM dragon.

And this is another component of the secret key to developing your early-stage start-up: Find your own dragon and invite innovators and disrupters to come along for the journey. *That* is how you compete with companies bigger and more powerful than you.

THE INSPIRING EXAMPLE OF DISNEY'S "WHY"

Roughly one hundred years ago, two brothers started an illustrating company. If you go back and look, you will find the phrase "Disney Brothers Illustrators" on their little business storefront. Today, we know how their story unfolded, but it is worth spending time with their purpose statement, which one can easily argue was the driving force behind their amazing story of growth and success. Simon Sinek invokes the Disney message often in his teachings.

Start by thinking for a moment about how someone from Disney would explain their company if asked. You might know someone from the company because it is so large, or you probably have run into a Disney employee at one of their parks. Take a moment and just *imagine* (a word that also invokes Disney) how they would respond if you asked them to tell you about the company. What would they say?

I can promise you that it is unlikely that you'd hear any Disney employee or other stakeholder responding by saying that the company builds and runs parks, makes movies, and creates pictures of a mouse. These are obviously components of Disney's revenue stream—as anyone with kids who demand a Disney vacation will know. But explaining what Disney does to make money is really not the point. It is always about *why*.

You are thus likely to hear that working at Disney involves focusing on bringing joy to families through storytelling. Sinek notes this point frequently in his own work. He has referred to Walt Disney as an eternal optimist and, while trying to grow the Disney company during the Great Depression of the 1930s, he did not celebrate the pain of everyday life but rather celebrated that life is about the joy and love of family.

What does this mean for your early-stage start-up? I hope by now that this should be obvious. If you can find something visceral in the belief system that drove you to create your company, then you can connect with early customers. And this belief system cannot be forced. It must be honest and authentic. "Why else," you must ask yourself, "would you commit your time and effort into something so crazy as a start-up?" You have to believe.

Memorize this: Revealing your belief system, assuming it is sufficiently inspiring, will attract early buyers. That is not conjecture. It is fact. Just ask the Disney brothers (well, you would have had to have asked them many decades ago, but you get the idea).

THE ILLUSTRATIVE EXAMPLE OF GOOGLE'S (SHIFTING) "WHY"

When I first saw the Google browser in 1998, I had difficulty understanding how it would replace the amazing AltaVista browser that I had been using successfully in my work at Bell Labs. AltaVista, for those of you who might not remember, was a popular early

Web browser used in the mid- to late 1990s. And it was every bit as amazing to use, at least in my observation, as Google is today.

Google Chrome is now miles ahead of those early browsers, but our expectation as users was lower then. AltaVista competed at the time with "Jerry and David's Guide to the World Wide Web," which was nothing more than a list of websites organized into categories (the site evolved into Yahoo!). I used AltaVista every day, but I had zero idea who the founders were or why they built their product. I just used the tool, and that's all. (Keep that point in mind.)

But when I eventually became aware of Google, something struck me as both amazing and inspiring, and it was the belief system of the two young computer science students who served as founders. They said that their company was founded on the principle of not being evil. Yes, they said that the company was created based on this belief: Don't be evil. In fact, the phrase became the rallying cry for Googlers, and I loved it.

Here was a start-up company founded on an idea that you could really connect with—and for technology companies, this was more than a small step forward. It was a giant leap forward. To this day, I still think of this as one of the best "why" statements for a company that I've ever seen. And everyone I worked with, in fact, everyone I knew, began to shift away from AltaVista and toward Google.

In the early days of web browsing, you could actually see evidence of this belief system in the query results you'd get from Google. If you were searching the Internet, for example, for the coolest electric guitars with a 1960s twang, then you'd see a long series of links pointing to sites from guitar experts providing information on this topic. And you'd see these links organized using Google's page rank algorithm.

This now-famous approach counted the number of links to a given page and determined the quality of those links to develop a view of how important that site must be. But it was not until October 23, 2000, considered D-Day for many of us purists who still long for an ad-free Internet experience, when Google launched AdWords. This platform offered the world's first self-serve online advertising platform. And everything changed after that.

In fact, with this one decision, Google successfully *crossed* the chasm. It took only two years to get there—and the world has not been the same since. In fact, the decision to launch AdWords ultimately made Google rich. But on October 23, 2000, Google arguably became evil. Not strangle-people-with-piano-wire evil, or even cheat-you-with-bad-products evil. But evil enough from an online advertising perspective that "Don't be evil" no longer made sense.

Readers will understand that to cross the chasm into the early and late majority, Google had no choice but to make this decision as illustrated in figure 1.2. It understood what had to be done, and changes were made, arguably major ones, in how it interpreted its belief system. These early beliefs, as described above, had attracted early customers *like me*. But now Google needed to focus on the majority, and that demanded focusing on *what* they did—namely, organizing the world's information.

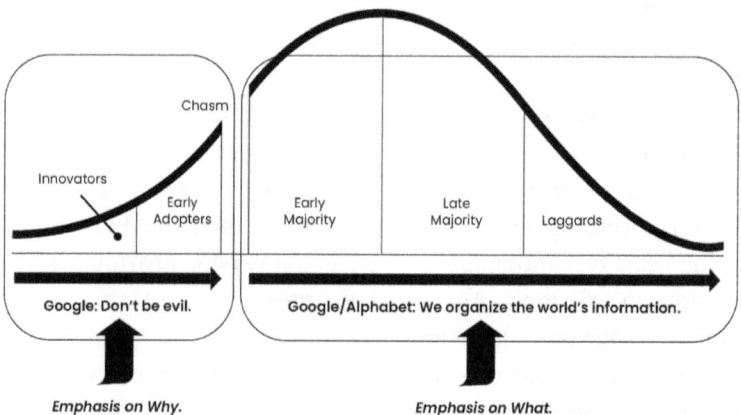

Figure 1.2 Google's journey toward and beyond the chasm

You can decide whether this was the right decision, but it's hard to imagine anyone disputing the call. It made Google the massive company it is today—and it underscores the shift from early adopter customers who focus on beliefs and early majority customers who focus on needs. I believe this to be one of the canonical examples of a company starting with a core belief system and then making some adjustments in order to scale.

When I bring up this case study during advisory sessions, founders always bring up what might seem obvious: "If Google had a true belief system, then how could that have changed? Isn't a belief system foundational? Were they just lying to all of us?" My answer is that the objective to not be evil never changed. Rather, it was the interpretation that changed. Not being evil in 1998 meant no ads. Not being evil in 2020 shifted to providing great searches.

Keep the Google example in mind: Your belief system should remain steady during your journey to the chasm, and it should not have to change much when it is time to begin scaling. But the interpretation of your belief system will probably change. Early-stage start-ups need not worry about this now, but it is worth anticipating—and it can help provide high-fidelity vision into the long-term prospects that lie ahead.

Google's decision to change its approach was the first step toward middle age for the company. The new purpose statement at the company—"We organize the world's information"—is obviously a description of what Google does, not why it does what it does. In fact, pundits and societal observers might argue that search engines have in fact become evil—and that generative AI tools will disrupt the entire business. Time will tell.

Google's board rebranded the parent company as Alphabet in 2015 and, in a note to customers, investors, and the world, Larry Page and Sergey Brin introduced the new entity with lines like this: "What is Alphabet? Alphabet is mostly a collection of companies." And they continued with lines like this: "Fundamentally, we believe this allows us more management scale, as we can run things independently that aren't very related."

Such statements are intentionally devoid of any semblance of purpose. They sound exactly like comments from a bureaucratic company. Even mature companies can reinvent themselves during maturity to perhaps become more like a start-up instead of a bureaucrat, and this process can resemble the belief-oriented approaches taken by start-ups.

For example, Alphabet might have said something like this when they created the new entity: "At Alphabet, we believe that the future lies in the hands of the inventor. And we've created an environment designed to invent the future." If I were coaching Alphabet (and yes, we continue to ask), I would have made this suggestion because that is their ethos.

And such a future purpose is something I could get excited about. I already had because that was what we believed at Bell Labs. We were inventing the future. When I went on my first interview at Bell Labs in 1984, I spoke with various members of the technical staff. Each would describe their work and ask me questions, but every interview ended with a statement of purpose about Bell Labs inventing the future.

Alphabet could have announced something like this: "At Alphabet, we believe in going to Mars. And we believe in using AI to reinvent our global society. And we believe in transforming every aspect of our lives for the better, through crazy, insane innovation. We believe in doing the unthinkable. And we do not believe in conventional organization. In fact, we like chaos. Alphabet is about inventing the future. Come with us on the journey."

Alphabet behaves instead like a company that has left its early years in the rearview mirror. They focus on what they do, and this serves both an early and late majority of buyers. They have even reached the stage where laggards are Google users. They are no longer a start-up—and when you have the market capitalization that they enjoy, I don't think you care. But time marches on, and Alphabet is getting old.

"WHY" STATEMENT CASE STUDY: AMENAZA

Now that we have looked at three of the biggest companies in the world, Apple, Disney, and Alphabet, let's look at one of the tiniest, with just two people. But I think you will enjoy hearing their story, which involved shifting from an emphasis on the engineering specifics of their technical analysis approach to one that focuses more on their mission and purpose. We doubt they will become the next Apple, but the shift in emphasis will drive them to growth.

The small company is called Amenaza, and it is run by a fine Canadian technologist named Terry Ingoldsby. He contacted me a couple of years ago to discuss how to grow his business. Terry specializes in something called threat modeling, a method of analyzing cybersecurity that I actually helped to invent in the 1980s on an old U.S. defense system called Star Wars. Terry has developed software that leveraged this method for complex systems.

When he and I began to discuss his business, you know what I asked him: "Tell me about your company." His answer, as one would expect from a good technologist, involved a crisp description of how his company performed attack tree-based risk modeling. It was a technically accurate and easy-to-follow description, but it was a statement of what he was doing versus an explanation of why his company existed in the first place.

We immediately started to explore how to adjust the messaging. In a series of advisory and coaching discussions with Terry and his business partner involving many hours of review, it became clear that there was an underlying premise behind everything he was doing as a security and technology expert: He believed, and his company was founded on that belief, that hostile behavior could be predicted.

Terry was suggesting, and I agreed, that security incidents did not have to be inevitable occurrences with no forewarning. Amenaza believed to its core that hacks, attacks, and other malicious acts were predictable. If his method was applied correctly to critically important systems, the result could prevent loss of life and ensure safer and more secure systems supporting our society.

Now *this* had some interesting implications that were much broader than the concerns of a small cybersecurity company. We worked with this idea and eventually came up with the concept that, when they were asked to talk about Amenaza, the company principals would always focus on their belief system and purpose—namely, that hostile behavior can be predicted and that such insight had significant potential benefit for the world.

If you ask Terry, he will tell you that this single adjustment in the company's purpose statement made more progress in a series of coaching sessions than they'd made previously over several years. We hope Terry succeeds wildly with this approach. Given the importance of Amenaza's mission, I suspect you will also be rooting (perhaps with your wallet) for their solution to grow in use across our world's most important and critical systems.

"WHY" STATEMENT CASE STUDY: TERRAFORMA

Let's look at another small company, one that operates in a different industry compared to Amenaza. We had the pleasure at TAG of working with a fine team of entrepreneurs, Brock Pollock, Jennifer Acevado, and Tyler Acevado from a start-up called TerraForma, a composting vendor focused on sustainability. Their approach to aerobic, organic waste recycling offers promise in addressing carbon emissions, and it has been a pleasure to work with these founders.

When you deal with start-up companies working in sustainability and climate science, they already begin with an amazing underlying purpose: to save the planet. It should be obvious that saving the planet is an excellent motivator for founders to decide to take the start-up plunge.

The problem is that, to *differentiate* from their competition, it is not enough for TerraForma to say that their purpose is to drive sustainability and lower carbon emissions. These are givens—so start-ups must use these drivers to tailor a more specific statement of belief and purpose.

As we worked with TerraForma, its principals were good at describing what they do and how their product works. They described in detail the advantages of their reduction cycle, their in-vessel aerobic approach, and the many uses for the organic compost output that their customers enjoy. This information flowed freely, and it was obvious that the company was taking this approach when pitching their solution to their own prospects.

Just as you would expect, our advisory sessions eventually focused on what really drove the company at its core and what comprised the belief system that served as a foundation for TerraForma. In a stray remark by one of the company founders during one of our strategy sessions, it became obvious what the TerraForma purpose statement should be.

Before I tell you what we came up with, I should mention that it is not always easy to spot a good "why" statement, especially for start-ups developing complicated solutions for specific types of applications. The vacuous tendency is to notice that if your product "does X," then perhaps your belief system is "do X." You must be careful not to fall into this trap. Rather, you need timeless statements of belief that transcend your actual product.

Here is what we heard from TerraForma. It is a statement of belief and purpose that we loved, and it struck us as a wonderful "why" statement for the company: "At TerraForma, we believe that nothing is trash." This statement came up during an advisory session, and it really popped out as both interesting and foundational to the company.

"We believe that nothing is trash". The more I stare at that statement, the more I see an innovative start-up that sees value where others see trash, that sees usefulness in debris, and that finds useful applications for things that normal people would just toss. It's the kind of belief system that helps you understand what other types of products and services TerraForma might offer. It's the beginning of a brand.

This is generally a good hint that you have a great belief statement. Could you change your product and keep the same belief statement? If the answer is yes, then you are on the right track. If the answer is no, then you really ought to take some time and determine what purpose is driving your start-up. Ask yourself what a hotel, a car, or a restaurant from your start-up would look like (assuming these are not your businesses). The answer should be obvious.

THE IMPORTANCE OF A FOUNDING STORY IN ESTABLISHING "WHY"

I've learned that the founding story for a start-up can often highlight its belief system. I noticed this phenomenon after several marketing teams, when pressed on their purpose, agreed to release (perhaps even momentarily) their insistence on describing what they do to focus more on their purpose. I noticed more than once that the discussion would eventually shift toward the founding story—and that's where things would finally get interesting.

I remember, for example, the security company Malwarebytes sharing the story of their founder Marcin Kleczynski. As a teenager in Poland, Kleczynski was furious that his mother's computer was infected with viruses. He vowed to fix the problem—and his work led him to create a start-up that now has thousands of customers, including perhaps you, located around the world. That is a fine purpose story—and certainly something a buyer could get excited about.

And now a little exercise for start-up founders and their teams. It begins with imagining the following scenario: If you had all the money that you could ever need, would you still be driving your start-up for growth, or would you be out on a golf course or a beach, or traveling? What would you be doing now if you did not need to work? As usual, I'd like you to think about this for a minute.

What did you come up with? If your answer is the golf course or the beach, then I honestly believe that you should not be a start-up founder. A start-up is like a child, and its parent, which is you, the founder, should be more focused on it than literally anything else in the world, like a good parent. (Being a start-up founder might make you a bad parent for your birth children; I'm sorry, but this is often true.)

The correct answer to the what-would-you-do question for the successful founder is that they would be knee-deep in their start-up. They would explain that not golf, beach vacations, or even traveling the world would come even marginally close to the rewards that come from chasing one's start-up dream. That is the fire in the belly required to be a successful founder. If your true motivation is the golf course, then quit the start-up and play golf.

My own founding story at TAG was that I had the best job in an amazing company with good prospects for longtime tenure. But something was missing. And I also had this nagging gut feeling that the research and advisory support from the massive legacy analyst firm, Gartner, was terrible and could be disrupted. This was not just the delusions of a founder but rather something confirmed by most of my colleagues.

In areas such as cybersecurity where human lives could be on the line (hackers do target critical infrastructure), bad advice was unacceptable. And I just knew that I could do better. That was my sincerely held belief. I felt this in my heart, and I had to find a way to follow this crazy dream of disrupting a multibillion-dollar industry. My wife thought I was nuts.

When your spouse thinks you're nuts, you're probably on the right track. And you must weave this into the founding story—as I just did. With my spouse's reluctant blessing, I stepped down from what I still think was the best job in the world, where I was making an excellent salary and had lifelong friends and colleagues, and I created a start-up. I had no revenue, no customers, no office, no employees.

The situation sounds crazy as I type these words because I was leaving a pampered life for the unknown. I did this not because I had a product idea (I had none), but I did hold the sincere belief that I could disrupt and improve on a vital aspect of cybersecurity. I just *knew* that I could do it. I decided to go after it. It was one guy—me—going after a six-billion-dollar company.

"Now," I often say to prospective early-adopter customers after relating my purpose-driven story, "would you like to come along with me on my journey to disrupt Gartner?" I can tell you that hundreds of major companies have decided that the answer is yes. So many have said yes that we have now expanded our research and advisory practice to include an exciting automated platform—with more to come.

AN EXERCISE TO DEVELOP A PROPER "WHY" STATEMENT

A useful exercise in developing a "why" statement involves selling your company with no mention of the product or service. For example, a company using AI to reinvent health care would not be allowed to mention AI, health care, or anything related to their platform. They would have to explain their story, draw an analogy, or invent some narrative that would lead a buyer to want to make a purchase.

I should say that when we do this exercise with TAG customers, they typically struggle. It's like asking a teenager to tell a story without using the words "um," "like," or "you know." We watch founders literally get tongue-tied trying to sell their company to us without mentioning their product. But in the end, 100 percent report that the exercise was useful—even if an acceptable answer is never reached (and this does happen).

I remember Kevin Mandia, founder of Mandiant and now a principal with Ballistic Ventures, explaining to me, back when I was his sales prospect, that he started his company because the Federal Bureau of Investigation (FBI) did not have the resources to help companies who had been hacked. These people needed a voice; they needed someone to help them—and Mandiant would be that company. He was right in his belief system, and Google recently paid $5.4 billion for the company.

Notice that when this founder explained his company, he never really got into what they were doing, as I recall. I remember him explaining his purpose and motivation. Apart from the fact that Kevin Mandia was and is the real thing, I believe that it was this purpose-driven belief system that led to the company's success.

Take some time and see if you can develop a statement about your company that does not mention your product and that expresses a belief system. Avoid statements that would remain true if your competition just cut-and-pasted their name into your claim. If, for example, McDonalds said that their mission was to deliver cheap food quickly, then a thousand other companies could make the same claim.

This type of statement is so urgent that you should get your management team together and work on something until you get it. Focus on why, not what. And you will soon see the impact as you measure your sales, revenue, and yes—even profitability. This is the key to getting an early-stage start-up off the ground—and I believe it is also the difference between companies that change the world and ones that burn for a time and then eventually extinguish.

After you have done this exercise, come back and read the next chapter, which focuses less on you and more on your customer.

2

WHAT IS YOUR VALUE PROPOSITION?

One hundred percent of the start-up founders I speak with every day, when asked about their value proposition, immediately provide a detailed description of some problem their customers have. They then explain how their unique offering, whether it is product, service, or platform, solves this problem in a way that no one else has considered or that existing vendors are attending to insufficiently.

"What is your value proposition?" we ask founders. And they always respond with this: "Here is the customer problem that we solve." We ask X, and they answer Y. It's like clockwork.

This is a perfectly reasonable view and, of course, your offering must match some customer need. If, for example, you provide SaaS-based support for developers needing access to AI-based models, then someone must *really need* this type of SaaS offering. Everyone understands this basic fact. But in my experience, solving a customer problem is insufficient as the primary value proposition for an early-stage company.

I have come to understand that, even with ample venture capital funding and an expert team given the luxury of developing in stealth, the value proposition of your early-stage company will not involve the functionality of the product. I believe that comes a bit later, once you have reached the chasm. I firmly believe that your value proposition, in your early stages, should center on the concept of *creating community*. Let me explain.

DELIVERING COMMUNITY TO EARLY ADOPTERS

As suggested above, any business textbook will explain that a value proposition is what a company delivers to its customers. For large companies, this can be straightforward—such as Heinz delivering extra thick ketchup or Procter & Gamble delivering a fresh smelling cleanser. For start-ups, however, the best value proposition involves providing an entry for buyers into a community—and that community should be based on a shared belief.

This is a powerful notion, one that cannot be underestimated. Start-ups inevitably offer inferior products—and yes, I know you are protesting as you read this. I know that you swear that your solution is better than the existing products, services, and platforms from legacy companies. I've heard this a thousand times and, on occasion, it might even be true. But the primary value proposition new companies can offer is acceptance into a new community.

This is how belief systems drive value propositions. It explains why people line up behind political leaders and why people stand in line for hours to see Bruce Springsteen for the thirtieth time. They are there because they want to feel part of something—and the best start-ups understand this and harness its power. Your value proposition for customers, during your early stage of development, will be more visceral than tangible. Remember this.

This concept should also apply to investors. Founding teams doing funding rounds, whether through angel, seed, series A, series B, or some later round, ask us for advice on how to create a value proposition that will drive a term sheet. Our answer is this: Developing a powerful value proposition for customers is, by definition, what venture capital teams want you to do. They are not looking to use your product; they want *others* to use your product.

Venture capital teams look for specific attributes that will be different from what buyers look for. For example, investors love founders who've been through prior exits. Buyers, in my experience, think somewhat differently. When you brag about the millions you got from Cisco or IBM, I think that angers buyers. No one wants to join a community with bragging rich founders. And the goal, again, should be *community*.

DEVELOPING YOUR BRAND

I've noticed that few if any start-up founders have thought much about establishing what might best be described as a brand. Most have no idea what is even meant by a good brand. They tend to think of brands as intangible attributes of large companies like Coca Cola and Nike and that the idea of developing a brand during the start-up phase is like putting the cart before the horse. This is wrong: You need to work on your brand from the outset.

This is not as easy as it sounds unfortunately, which is why it is skipped so often by start-up founders. I had the privilege to attend the Columbia Senior Executive Program (CSEP) at Columbia Business School, and I specifically remember during one lecture writing in my notes the word "brand" with a question mark after it. I don't think I've seen one presentation in the last five years from start-up founders that even used the word. It's viewed as out of scope.

When founders are inevitably turned off by my reference to development of a brand, I often suggest that they just substitute in the word *perception*. And I remind them that they have two choices: They can work to develop how they are perceived by customers, analysts, and investors, or they can just let their competition accomplish this task. There is no other option.

Let's examine a simple model to explain how this works. As we discussed in our first chapter, you have to stand for something. We called that a belief system. And we explained, we hope convincingly, that you need to try to attract your early customers by having them connect with your belief system. We showed that such visceral attraction can be powerful enough to set aside the irrationality of buying from an early-stage vendor.

But here is where it gets interesting. This wonderful feeling of buying something that connects with your own belief system is the value proposition your customers feel when they buy from you in the early stages of your development. Even after your start-up has grown larger, this idea that buying from you "says something" about who I am as a buyer is like rocket fuel if you get it right.

We can explain this concept in three steps. First, the start-up *defines* its belief system. Our favorite is the Steve Jobs approach of slaying a big dragon, but it is whatever you have made it. At TAG, we are going after Gartner, which we believe deserves to be disrupted. Second, you *attract* buyers who possess your shared belief. They might agree with Jobs that IBM is too big and too impersonal. Never mind that IBM makes computers a thousand times better than the early Apple machines. That is irrelevant.

Third, once your initial customers have purchased your minimum viable product (MVP) and begin installing subsequent fixed versions of your offering, they become part of a de facto community. I'm not talking about them meeting with you and other customers for picnics—although the creation of regional user groups is a great idea. I am talking about a more visceral level. When they buy from you, they are expressing a belief, and that is what we mean by "community."

As illustrated in figure 2.1, buyers are attracted to start-ups who can create a community of shared belief. That word, "community," is one that you should remember. It is the basis for the best value propositions. Buyers want to feel that, when they buy from you, they are part of something. This is more important than solving a customer problem, which is a given, but it will not be enough, especially in areas where the competition is fierce.

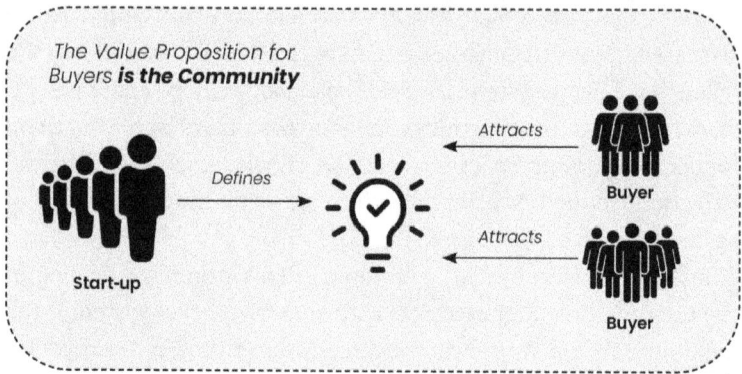

Figure 2.1 Shared belief systems lead to communities

LARGE COMPANY BRANDS: THE EXAMPLE OF SOUTHWEST

We've already mentioned Apple and Disney—two of the greatest brands ever developed. When you purchase an Apple device, you are saying something about yourself. And when you spend a week on vacation at a Disney park, you are also saying something about yourself. The opposite also holds. When you avoid buying Microsoft or when you choose to not vacation at adults-only beaches in Jamaica, that also says something about you.

Let's look at Southwest Airlines. If you share a generation with me, then you still connect this company with its amazing cofounder Herb Kelleher. During its early years, Southwest was known as the company where employees never took themselves seriously and worked to create an environment of fun. But the company was also dead serious in its execution, with *Fortune* magazine naming it as among the most admired companies in the United States in 2018.

My personal experience with the company and its famous (former) brand is consistent with the above, although not always to optimal effect. I was once on a business flight from Denver to Seattle during Kelleher's tenure, and after a tiring and unproductive day of meetings, I slumped into a seat at the front of the plane (Southwest has open seating). I remember that I wanted to be left alone to sleep off a tough day.

As we pushed off the gate, one of the cheerful Southwest flight attendants must have noticed my surly mood. He got onto the microphone and made a loud public announcement that everyone on the plane needed to give a big: "Awwww" to Mr. Grumpy who was seated up here in 1A. I remember glancing up at the attendant and, then suddenly, to my horror, it became clear that Mr. Grumpy was in fact *me*. Not a great moment, but it reinforced their brand.

What is the brand you associate with Southwest now? Since Kelleher's retirement and death in 2019, the company seems different. I suspect this is unfair to say because I guess they remain a good company. The stock seems to have performed okay since the Kelleher days, so business pundits might call my comments unfair. And I am not a financial analyst so don't take any of my comments here as guidance for investors.

But any observer would have to admit that its string of information technology (IT) disasters, combined with the loss of its charismatic founder, has left Southwest somewhat unmoored in terms of their brand. When I think of Southwest today, I just think of an airline, perhaps with low fares. If I was on their board of directors, I'd be recommending the hiring of some zany new spokesperson and I'd dial up once again the employee spirit and brand of fun and enjoyment.

DESCRIBING YOUR PRODUCT (BUT BE CAREFUL)

Ask a founder about their product, and it's like asking a soccer Dad about his daughter's goal-scoring ability. Both start-up founder and doting father will offer a long narrative with loads of detail and considerable gushing pride. While having a great product is table stakes, obviously, for getting customers to sign up and then renew, being overly focused on one's product can be a handicap. And yes, you can be overly focused on the product.

This is a weird concept, one that is not easy to explain during advisory sessions with founders. Consider what I just said: Being overly focused on describing your product with enthusiasm and ease could actually be a liability. How could that possibly be?

The problem is that, if you as founder are so good at describing your product—your baby, so to speak—then you will do so at every possible occasion and opportunity, readily and willingly. As we've suggested above, however, you should be much more focused as a founder of a start-up on purpose and on community. Both are visceral, and both are intended to attract buyers to an idea versus to your more tangible offering.

But this is not the comfort zone for most founders—and probably not for you. For example, if you were asked to talk about your start-up in front of a large audience or during some other high-profile, high-stress event, you'll revert to your comfort zone if you are like most founders, and if that involves describing your product instead of your belief system, then this is what you will do. We see this as a problem for start-ups.

We fully understand that a successful start-up involves an entire team, not just the founding group—and this team includes sales engineers, marketing team members, and others who will spend a great deal of time being asked to describe the value proposition. You might find this surprising, but our advice to the rest of the company is no different than what we offer to the CEO—and it is this:

> Everyone in an early-stage start-up should be obsessed with sharing the details of the company's purpose and reason for being. These are more important than the functionality of your product in establishing an early buying base.

A major hint about why you should focus on purpose over function seems obvious: The rate of change regarding reinvention, redesign, and rebuild for start-ups is usually high. That's the whole idea of the nimble start-up, which can change direction quickly. If you spend all your time explaining how awesome the interface is to your cloud-based service, then that is true until it isn't true anymore. And with start-ups, functionality and features change fast.

I understand that the conventional wisdom is to define one's value proposition via descriptions of the product or service functionality using template PowerPoint presentations that quote their Gartner category (ugh), including colorful diagrams of the architecture or solution setup (double ugh), with a path to lead the prospect to sit through some sort of demonstration (triple ugh).

If you stick with this lukewarm and conventional approach to defining your value proposition, you will have lukewarm and conventional sales results. Maybe write that one down to remember: Following conventional wisdom will get you lukewarm results.

Unless explicitly requested by a prospect, demos should not be used at the front end of building a relationship. For early-stage start-ups, it is best to delay showing demos for as long as you can. Executives should also never be shown demos, even if they ask. Remember that executives will not understand the nuances of any functional improvements you've introduced over your competitor's solution. They'll just look at the pretty colors.

More times than I can hardly believe, a sales team will be incented to do demos for anyone who will sit and listen. Perhaps the sales leadership team even keeps track of the number of demos done. And sometimes, demos are actually done on sales calls after the customer has already agreed to a proof of concept (POC). This stubborn insistence on doing a demo introduces the potential that you might snatch a no answer from the jaws of a yes answer.

We understand that founders and other principals in a start-up are eager to prove that they actually have something—hence, the demo. We get that you previously had only PowerPoint and now that you have a product, you are proud to demonstrate it to the world. That is human nature. But please resist. Buyers already assume that you have something or they would not take your call. Let your solution live in their imagination as long as you can.

Demos are obviously essential when a start-up has begun crossing the chasm to a larger mainstream buying group. Once your innovator and early adopter customer markets have been sufficiently mined, then you will need to realign your strategy around developing a solution that matches the needs of this large group. Once this occurs, you will begin to make the transition from early stage to more mature stage—and demos will be essential.

CASE STUDY IN PRODUCT FLEXIBILITY:
ATTIVO NETWORKS

My longtime friend Tushar Kothari founded Attivo Networks in 2011 with the goal of using clever deception as a means for tricking an adversary into getting caught on a corporate IT network. His product originally involved a virtual lure or trap on company systems, and I loved the idea. I used it to help secure massive telecommunications infrastructure, and after I started TAG, I continued to follow their progress.

You might be surprised to know that, by 2022, when Kothari's company was bought by SentinelOne for over $600 million, Attivo Networks barely mentioned deception in its marketing. The core belief system of the company had not changed, but its customer interests, needs, and preferences had changed dramatically in the eleven years that Kothari ran Attivo, and he was flexible enough to understand this and to adapt as he transitioned to a larger buying group.

I spent quite a bit of time with the Attivo team from 2016 to 2022, writing articles, supporting webinars, and interviewing Kothari for our YouTube channel. In all these interactions, I was always struck by how the company celebrated its purpose, which was to block or slow down the progression of attacks. Attivo was like a safety shield that diverted an attack once it had commenced.

A big part of the original Attivo approach involved using the deception to stop hackers from exploiting weaknesses in Microsoft's Active Directory. Over time, this aspect of the solution became its greatest asset. As buying patterns in cybersecurity shifted and as the company grew, its success in emphasizing deception to buyers waned, just as interest in how to secure Active Directory soared.

As you might expect, Attivo took advantage of this. If you review the work done by its chief marketing officer at the time, Carolyn Crandall, you'll see that the company shifted its functional story expertly. Before long, Attivo was emphasizing its Active Directory protection, often with little or no reference to deception. This was quite an expert shift and something to admire as it unfolded.

It was a master class in crossing the chasm but doing so in a way that did not compromise the company's belief systems or value proposition to customers. The "what" changed for Attivo, but the "why" and "how" never budged. It should be clear that if the Attivo approach had been to emphasize "what" it did originally versus "why," then a shift in its product would not have been possible. SentinelOne wanted the safety net, not the deception, part of the story.

BUILDING YOUR CUSTOMER EXPERIENCE: SELF-SERVICE

The one value proposition–related topic that comes up most often in conversations with founders is customer experience. I am told repeatedly by founders that customer experience is key to their success and that they coach their teams to be customer obsessed. I am not 100 percent sure I understand what that means, but I've heard Jeff Bezos say multiple times that customer obsession was the key to developing Amazon. Who am I to argue with him?

When we get to the specifics of what is meant by customer experience, things get a tad more complex. First, we should recognize that the customer experience should include the totality of your interactions, starting with the sales cycle and leading to the deployment process. Customer experience also obviously includes the usage time line as well as the stages leading to retirement or replacement of the product.

Keep product retirement in mind because if a customer exits your early-stage product, that does not mean they are gone forever. Many buyers depart because they are more comfortable using established products. When you hit that stage, you can reach back to the former customer. Helping a customer comfortably retire usage of your MVP might even bring them back when you have something more mature.

This illustrates nicely that every aspect of the life cycle is an important part of the experience that you provide to your customers. As you might expect, this is where you can make a huge difference in terms of your value proposition over competitors. But this is where we start to hear about scaling to growth, which inevitably leads to the question of whether a given solution, for example, can include a self-service option for clients, which can translate to less cost, less friction, and more scale.

Almost every start-up we work with refers to this goal of creating a scalable customer experience that minimizes the totality of human support necessary. While this is an admirable goal, we always try to remind our clients that this can be done well, but it can also be done poorly. And when customers are asked to pick up the heavy lifting in a badly conceived self-service approach, things can get bad very fast.

Here's a brick-and-mortar example. Many department stores now try to minimize the number of people on the floor. Buyers are expected in these stores to follow a self-service routine of locating sizes, colors, and styles of clothing by wandering around and flipping through racks, hoping to find something to try on and then head for the dressing room. It might take a couple of minutes of looking, but customers eventually find the dressing room (usually near the bathroom).

This customer experience is usually not terrible, but it is also not great. And one wonders how it might be improved without the need to introduce a lot of employees back into the mix. One approach, for example, might be to use technology to enhance the experience. An app, for instance, could help buyers learn what clothing inventory exists in the store. It could help locate what they need based on their input into the app.

I've often thought about this and wonder why traditional companies avoid accelerating their customer experience in this manner, and I honestly do not have an answer. Perhaps it's the cost of development, the jolt of a changing mindset, and so on. But for start-ups, the laggard approaches that characterize legacy firms is good news for any team trying to develop a brand-new solution. Disrupting the old-fashioned customer experience is a great driver for start-ups.

BUILDING AN INITIAL CUSTOMER EXPERIENCE: THE CONCIERGE APPROACH

For early-stage companies, we coach them to be as helpful as possible and to offer their early customers the most amazing experience. The goal should be for the customers to have to do nothing except enjoy the experience. Uber does this so well. For example, if I am headed from some location in New York to one of the New York University (NYU) buildings where I teach, then I have many options. I could use the subway, which would be cheap, but super-hot in the summer and usually pretty noisy.

A second option would be to walk, which is healthy but takes some time. The third option is to tap into my Uber app, and within a minute or so, a car pulls up, I hop into the back, and without saying a word, the driver takes me to the front of my building. I hop out without having to do a single thing. The payment is automatic. This is self-service done perfectly—and it is something to emulate.

For your own start-up, what would be the version of the Uber experience that would makes your customers feel like their experience was special? Think hard because this fundamentally influences your "how" statement. It is a great way to differentiate and, during your early stages, do not worry about scale. Do whatever it takes to delight your early customers. You will figure how to scale later. For now, focus on providing a concierge experience.

One interim stop on your journey is that you must find one or more awesome reference customers. It's best if these references can involve big-name companies with big budgets and big reputations to provide sufficient buying cover for your later mass-market prospects. These big customers want start-up concierge treatment—and you should cheerfully comply. You'll be glad that you attended to this step when you reach the chasm.

That's an important point and one to reinforce: You will need to grab one or more big reference clients during your early-stage growth. Concierge treatment is a great way to do that.

BUILDING YOUR CUSTOMER EXPERIENCE:
TRY HARDER

I am often asked how in the world a little start-up can beat a bigger company—and one of my favorite answers is also my simplest answer: It can try harder. I know this might sound a bit obvious, but it is more subtle than you might think. And it plays into the collective psyche, moods, and opinions of your initial buyers. Show them that you are clawing away 24/7 to reach a target fueled by a belief system, and they will join you on the journey.

We have found that a great motivation for a start-up to want to try harder involves its desire to slay some corporate dragon. As I alluded to previously, we often ask our customers at TAG to help us slay the huge Gartner dragon. We refer to ourselves informally as the unGartner, and this usually gets our early prospects excited. We ask if they would like to come along with us on the journey—and they often say yes.

When you take this route, you create an experience for your customers in which they participate actively in your business. They feel like a partner in the process, and this will excuse bugs or other warts in your early offering. It is a powerful way to gain traction when you know you cannot honestly re-create what the larger competing entity can do. This is the Steve-Jobs-giving-the-finger-to-the-IBM-sign approach. It truly involves just plain trying harder.

Do you remember Avis doing this to Hertz? The concept was memorialized in a quirky delightful book from the Avis CEO called *Up the Organization*. The book explained how Avis was going to try harder—that was the advertising slogan: "We try harder." People often point to Apple as being the first modern company that tried to think differently to gain customers. For my money, it was Avis.

START-UP CUSTOMER EXPERIENCE: CYBERWA CASE STUDY

If you work in cybersecurity, then you know Will Pelgrin. As driver of a nonprofit known as the Center for Internet Security (CIS), Will led development of a security framework used by companies hoping to improve their cybersecurity. If you get the chance to meet Will, you will find someone 100 percent committed to service. Before leading CIS, Will served New York State as a cybersecurity coordinator, and his impact to the citizens of that state was considerable. He is quite the role model.

Will called me several years ago explaining that he was providing concierge cyber-services for high-net-worth individuals, executives, and celebrities to protect their online digital personas as well as those of their family members and close associates. Will's team of experts was being made available to clients, with the agreement that they cooperate and share their online personas with the CyberWA team.

Customers of CyberWA experience a level of service that is unimaginable, at least with respect to their online protection. When something happens to them online, if they suspect that something might be amiss with an account or device, or if they have a question about their Wi-Fi, they can reach out to CyberWA, and an expert will be there. This does not scale, but that is not the point. Instead, the goal is reference customers, and CyberWA certainly has that.

Our coaching to Will and his CyberWA team, as you might expect, has been that the company should continue to use this amazing level of service to focus on their richest clients who can pay the highest fees. The next phase, should the company decide to move in this direction, is to focus on the chasm. That will be a decision they will have to make because scaled growth will demand an adjusted model.

Will's company illustrates something I hope every founder reading this book will consider: If you have the option to stick with innovators and early adopters, then this can be a nice life. Investors refer to this (often somewhat dismissively) as a lifestyle business. Obviously, if you've taken $20 million in series A, then this is not an option. Your investors want you to reach and eventually cross the chasm. That's the life you chose.

But for everyone else, including you brave souls who might have bootstrapped your company (and I am one), there is absolutely no reason why you must try to scale to high growth. If you enjoy your early customer base, then give yourself the option to spend time delighting that base. It's a nice life and can sometimes offer a more purpose-driven connection to your customers than growing to a big public company.

VALUE PROPOSITION = BRAND + PRODUCT + EXPERIENCE

Let's put this all together. I fundamentally believe that your value proposition sits at the intersection, perhaps best represented using a Venn diagram, of your company brand, your product offering, and your customer experience. When these are all well conceived and carefully thought out, and when they align nicely with your customer base, then you've got yourself a nice value proposition.

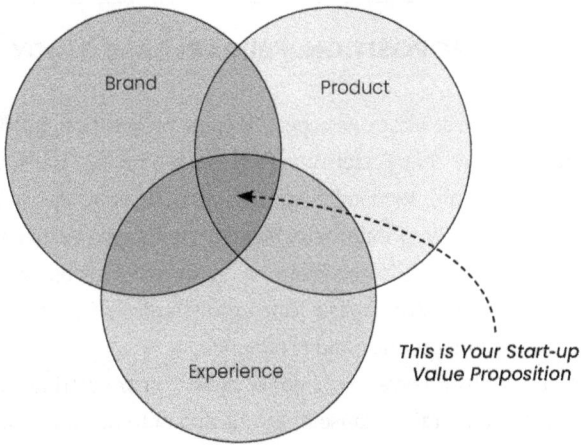

Figure 2.2 Value proposition model

As illustrated in figure 2.2, the best strategy for a start-up to deliver benefit to customers is to focus on three objectives: Identify and reinforce a brand based on shared belief, deliver a disruptive product that connects with innovators and early adopters, and create a concierge experience that will stand in sharp contrast to larger and more established competitors. The resulting value proposition will sustain growth to the chasm.

I hope venture capital team readers will pay attention to these three steps in their interactions with start-ups. As I suggested at the outset of this chapter, I believe that they tend to make too big a deal out of the problem being solved by a founding team. "What problem are you solving?" they ask. And I've watched over and over as the founder heads off in the wrong direction, focusing too much on the product and not enough on community.

Your value proposition emerges from your brand based on belief, your product based on disruption, and your customer experience based on concierge. The result is that early-stage buyers adopting your solution become part of a community.

VALUE PROPOSITION: FERRARI CASE STUDY

To help illustrate at least one aspect of value proposition, let's look at Ferrari. I know that Ferrari is clearly not a start-up, but it is an instructive example. Remember that the actions you take and the business strategies you follow can be applicable in many non-start-up contexts. The trick in reaching the chasm involves picking and choosing the right path toward scaled growth. Ferrari offers useful insight into brand, product, and experience.

When you buy a Ferrari, it is not because you are getting a good deal. You buy a Ferrari because it is your dream to buy a Ferrari. As this book goes to press, its website shows a middle-aged guy looking at his financial statements, presumably to determine if a Ferrari is a possibility. The implication is that a Ferrari is something you earn, something you aspire to, and presumably something expensive. A Ferrari is a show-off car.

Ferrari's value proposition is surprisingly illustrative for start-ups. Their brand is synonymous with an expensive luxury purchase. Any item outside the context of cars can be referenced with respect to Ferrari. That is, any type of product, from restaurants to consulting services, to medical devices can be the Ferrari of its category. A basketball hoop, for example, that is the Ferrari of basketball hoops is the best basketball hoop. That is a brand.

The product is obviously disruptive and appeals to innovators and early adopters. By design, Ferrari does not sell to a mass market. And this is an interesting case study in certain sectors such as luxury brand companies operating very much like start-ups. I've always found this interesting because the last thing Ferrari would ever hope for would be to sell to a mass market. It would kill the brand.

The Ferrari customer experience is 100 percent first class. Emphasis during the concierge experience is on personalization, customization, and inclusion in an exclusive community of owners. Ferrari owners take pride in private access to limited-edition models, and the VIP treatment they receive from the company and its authorized dealerships. If you had to use one word to describe the Ferrari experience for customers, it would be exclusivity.

Combining these three things (personalization, customization, and exclusivity), you have the Ferrari value proposition: an amazing brand that implies luxury. A product that is top in performance, design, styling, and technology. A customer experience that spells exclusivity. These elements comprise the value proposition that has nothing to do with some problem being solved. A Ferrari is a dream—and the value proposition is wrapped in this basic fact.

VALUE PROPOSITION: HYUNDAI CASE STUDY

When you purchase a Hyundai, you tell the world that you are sensible. And the Hyundai brand has come to mean something. For example, companies often refer to themselves as being the Hyundai of their industry. A hotel, stadium, or even business suit might be the Hyundai of their category. The association is with reasonable cost and good quality. When you buy a Hyundai, you definitely say something about yourself.

Let's examine the Hyundai value proposition: The first pillar is brand, which involves achieving excellent value at an acceptable cost. Their website reinforces this message of saving money, getting good deals, and buying value at a low cost. This is a nice approach for vehicles. But it might not work in other cases, such as for specialized heart surgery, where a patient will want only the very best, regardless of cost.

The second pillar is product, and Hyundais are clearly well-made vehicles that achieve what they claim to achieve. This is key because, under any set of reasonable product comparison criteria, a Ferrari will always beat a Hyundai in terms of the capabilities included in the product. No one buying a Hyundai, however, laments this difference. Some Hyundai buyers celebrate (or even lampoon) the difference.

The third pillar is customer experience—and this conjures up the image of a driver smiling while driving on a highway as they whiz along in their Hyundai, confident in the fact that they saved a ton of money. Rather than offering a curated, red-carpet experience, the Hyundai value proposition is more visceral. It really does conjure up the feeling of pride that comes with saving money and getting a good deal.

One important warning, however, does emerge regarding the Hyundai approach: The last thing any early-stage start-up needs is to get involved in a so-called race to the bottom with its competitors. This refers to a pricing war that emerges between comparable providers who take turns lowering prices repeatedly until there is no deeper place to go—namely, they have hit the bottom.

While start-ups might have the ability to price lower than the more established option (especially true for services), the decision to go lower should be done only if absolutely required. We see quite a few start-ups in our work at TAG who use rock-bottom pricing or even free offers as an enticement to gain early adopters. I wish I could say that there is a hard-and-fast rule about whether this works, but there isn't one.

But don't overthink this. If you can charge more with your early adopter customers, then do it. Scale can come later.

START-UP VALUE PROPOSITION: SPHERE CASE STUDY

Cybersecurity start-up SPHERE has a solid value proposition for business customers, and it all comes from their founder Rita Gurevich. I first became aware of the company's founder through alumni programs at the Stevens Institute of Technology where she and I are both graduates (I received my PhD in computer science there). We eventually connected through her fine venture capital backers, ForgePoint, and we have been working together since.

The SPHERE value proposition is based on a brand that originated during the founder's time spent in financial services. She recognized how messy certain aspects of cybersecurity could be in a large bank, and she parlayed this into a services company that focused on cyber-hygiene. After years of doing this, she learned how it could be automated into a platform—and thus was born SPHERE. It came from practitioner experience, and it is focused on practitioner needs.

The SPHERE brand begins and ends with a deep understanding of the real needs of enterprise security teams. The company has a product that is practical, an ethos that matches the enthusiasm found in corporate environments, and a customer experience that is curated to ensure excellent results. It is a truly solid value proposition—and a master class in how to parlay corporate experience into a start-up that sells back into corporations.

But SPHERE is also a wonderful example of a company that understands the value of balancing products *and* services. It recognized early that connecting with innovators and early adopters demands a curated concierge experience—and this often implies the need to work closely with clients through provision of services. I have watched them do this, and it is an important part of their value proposition.

Many start-up founders try to jump too quickly to the chasm, however, and tell us that they worry about their valuation if they include services—and this is wrong. During the early stages of growth, the customer experience is a massive component of the value proposition; if you try too hard to be like Amazon or Uber, then you have missed the reason your customers have come to you in the first place. They want connection with a start-up, not scale.

If you have allowed your funding sources to drive you to focus on products and platforms that scale, then perhaps you are making a mistake we see too often: Start-up founders often stand at the base of a mountain and see the summit. They see where they want to be, but they often ignore the long and difficult path that will get them there. And for many of these companies, this implies the need to include services.

3

WHO ARE YOUR CUSTOMERS?

Start-ups, especially in business to business (B2B), often do not *understand* their target customers. This practice of figuring out who your customers are or will be is a neglected art. And by this, I mean *really* understanding the buyers of your early-stage product. If done correctly, this task involves figuring out their tendencies. You should know their interests, their buying habits, their aspirations, and who they are—as *human beings*.

This is a somewhat different exercise for business-to-consumer (B2C) start-ups, where the buyer belongs to a crowd versus working for a targeted company. But in either case, you must do whatever is necessary to understand your buyer. And as we have explained, start-up buyers tend to gravitate toward disruptive and innovative solutions. That should be your starting point in understanding their psyche. But be careful not to allow it to be your ending point.

Several years ago, I participated in a marketing exercise where a group of subjects was asked to describe what a large telecom would look like *as a person* versus what a small start-up might look like if it were also a person. It was a weird sort of anthropomorphic exercise, but the results were interesting and helped to identify the persona of buyer that each company might expect to find in their current customer mix.

One answer involved the picture of a young vibrant student with a backpack and sunglasses walking through a posh urban neighborhood sipping a drink and smiling, perhaps excited at the prospects for the future. The other answer involved the picture of an older gentleman wearing a sweater and smoking a pipe, looking comfortable and wise but also somewhat worn. I will let you guess which picture corresponded to which company.

Start-up teams would be wise to perform this exercise for their target customers. It can be done for a B2C crowd or a B2B company. It is especially useful for start-up founders who might not share a generation with their buyers. For example, if you are about the same age as the grandchildren of the decision makers leading a business you'd like to sell your product to, then you should acknowledge this explicitly. They must be treated accordingly.

UNDERSTANDING TRIBES

Remember that, whether you are selling to a business or to a crowd, you are dealing with people. Start-ups, especially technically minded ones, tend to forget this golden rule of sales: Human beings buy from other human beings. More specifically, humans buy from humans they like, who *believe* what they believe and who can deliver a value proposition that connects with their hopes and dreams (like owning a Ferrari).

I am not ashamed to admit that every time I tap on my iPhone, a tiny bit of me acknowledges that I was influenced in this decision by Steve Jobs. And every time I open Microsoft 365 to grab my email, I acknowledge that I was also probably influenced in that decision by Bill Gates. It's the same thing for Amazon, Netflix, and other services. This idea that we humans buy from other humans would seem to work just as well for B2C offerings.

At TAG, we have experimented with many methods to help new B2B start-ups conceptualize and operationalize this task of understanding their early customers—and we eventually settled on the notion of tribe. Our view is that every customer type, including B2C crowds, can be categorized into tribes and that by understanding the tribe of buyer interested in your product, you can do a better job tailoring the message to the sales opportunity.

A tribe is a collection of individuals with a common interest, purpose, and culture. Lawyers, doctors, teachers, marines, and accountants are examples of tribes that can be pitched to similarly —but *within the tribe*. For example, if you are selling financial consulting services, then you would approach doctors and lawyers one way, but you would pitch to teachers and marines in a much different manner.

Remember that this changes when you cross the chasm. The tailored pitch model is essential for a start-up market, but it is less important for a mass market. Microsoft, for example, does not change its value proposition for Microsoft 365 when dealing with accountants, lawyers, or software developers. These are mass-market buyers who purchase what they need versus what they believe. Many of these buyers now hate Microsoft but still purchase their products.

In the future, with AI-based selling solutions, it is possible that even large companies selling to a mass market will use intelligent algorithms to tailor their sales message to a tribe. But for now, you should keep the following in mind: Start-ups must understand the tribes of the buyers who will invest in their early-stage solutions. If you want to connect with buyers based on shared belief systems, then obviously you will need to know what your buyers believe.

CHAMPION AND APPROVER

For B2B start-ups, the sales process usually begins with someone falling in love with the start-up. This falling in love is weird to discuss with founders because it is usually so far outside their comfort zone. But we always remain firm about emphasizing this important fact: Any start-up sale to a business begins with some person falling in love with your company. And this love will be rooted in a shared belief rather than in your product.

The buyer will also feel awkward about admitting their affection for your company. They will inevitably reference certain features and the functionality of your solution. It is your interface or your excellent update routines or your shiny packaging, they will say, that justifies their use of your solution. This sounds good, and it makes it easier for them to justify an initial purchase, but it is their love that drives the initial sale, not functionality.

When this connection occurs, the start-up will have what's known as a champion. That champion will sell the value of the start-up to other individuals and groups within the company. I cannot give you a formula for finding a champion, but I can tell you this: Every champion holds a shared belief system with the start-up with which they've connected. That belief system is deep, and it sometimes even leads to statements from champions such as "I love that company."

A champion is so valuable because, just like in any other loving relationship, they will look the other way when your product develops warts. They will excuse the occasional blip in how your solution operates as long as they see you working hard and continuing to improve. But step away from the core belief system, such as becoming evil when you previously were not, and watch as the champion leaves you for another start-up. Keep that in mind.

Let's repeat this: Any champion attracted to your start-up through shared belief will leave you if your belief system changes. This might be inevitable once you reach the chasm, but having it happen before reaching the chasm is inadvisable.

In B2B, a second sale must typically be made that goes beyond the purchasing authority and responsibility of the champion, and it involves someone known as the approver. This is usually someone with the responsibility of managing and approving budget requests. In the typical case, the champion must convince the approver that a purchase from the start-up is a good idea. The champion is often

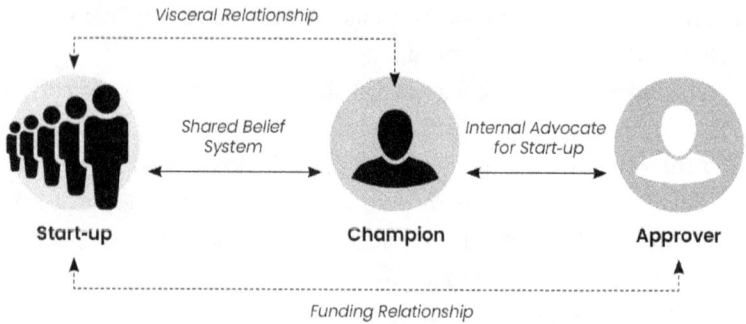

Figure 3.1 Roles of champions and approvers in start-up selling

a practitioner, and the approver is often a manager or executive—as illustrated in figure 3.1.

The simplest case occurs when the champion and approver are the same person. But the most complex case emerges when these two roles are filled with people from different tribes. Maybe your champion is a nurse in a hospital who went to nursing school and focuses 100 percent on patient health. The approver, however, might be a stodgy hospital administrator who went to business school and focuses 100 percent on costs. They must be approached differently.

Suppose, for example, that your start-up offers cool new technology that revolutionizes how restaurant kitchens are cleaned by using robots. Your champion would be the kitchen worker whose life would improve by having such robotic cleanup support. The approver, in contrast, will be the person who manages the money. A problem emerges when the approver considers replacing the champion with your product.

In cybersecurity, this phenomenon occurs with start-ups trying to automate the security operations process. Such tools will certainly look attractive to security staff working in an enterprise protection group. But it gets awkward when the approving entity, usually the chief information security officer (CISO), sees the product as perhaps reducing staff on the security operations team. Navigating these situations complicates the B2B sales process indeed.

COMMON TRAITS OF BUYING TRIBES

While every B2B start-up must differentiate between champions and approvers, this is not what we mean when we refer to tribes of buyers. To identify the tribe of any buyer, we must determine the defining characteristics or traits that the members of a particular tribe have in common. We have found four specific general traits—interest, background, aspirations, and culture—as good defining characteristics of a tribe to which you might be selling your B2B product or service.

Keep in mind that with both champions and approvers in the sales loop, you will probably have to make this tribal determination twice. If you are supporting a briefing, you should determine the tribe of everyone who will be present in advance (explained later in this chapter). For early start-ups, this task is especially critical because they will need to connect with their buyer on a more visceral level than after they have grown to a larger mass-market customer base.

Let's look at a couple of examples. First, teachers have a deep interest in the learning environment, and they work hard to create a nurturing culture in their classrooms. If you sell to teachers, then you should focus on this common trait. If you talk to them, for example, about your product helping them get a promotion or raise, then your message will likely fall flat. You have to understand the traits of the tribe in order to connect.

A second example could be lawyers, who often thrive in a culture of career ambition, starting with the need to succeed in law school. If you are selling to lawyers, then you should show them how your solution can help drive their careers forward. It should be obvious that if you focus your selling with lawyers on learning and nurturing, as you did with teachers, then it will fall flat. Again, you must understand the traits of your buying tribe.

Buyer Interests

The most obvious tribal trait involves a shared common interest, and this is probably the easiest way to define a tribe. As shown above for teachers and lawyers, the work activity associated with their profession generally offers an excellent means for defining the common interests of the group. If you are selling to accountants or to physicians, then the specifics of their tradecraft will always serve as a common point of discussion with the group.

But things do vary—and we have found a spectrum of common interests that ranges from deep technical issues to broad management approaches. Software environments, for example, include the developers who are interested in products, platforms, and services that connect with their daily software tasks, whereas their managers will be interested in ways to reduce head count, overhead, and time-to-deliver features.

Suppose that your start-up is approaching a business to sell them AI software. You identify a potential champion in the company who is deeply interested in AI technology, including how models and algorithms work. Your interactions with this champion should be awash in technical information, learning materials, and research results that will attract this champion based on their common interest with your team.

I like the idea in this example of lining up your most competent technical staff member with this champion, perhaps to discuss the finer points of how AI technology is used. These individuals can form a bond that we hope will result in the champion deciding that your start-up has a common belief system. In the best case, the champion falls in love with your company.

Let's suppose that you now encounter the approver, who has fundamentally different interests, perhaps more in the business or even societal aspects of the use of AI. As you interact with this approver, you'd be wise to set aside the technical details and offer a higher-level view of how your AI solution is responsible for business and that it will help the approver develop instincts around AI usage with a minimum of risk.

I like the idea here of the start-up founder or even the venture capital investor connecting with the approver to discuss some aspect of the business relationship. This works amazingly well if the venture capital investor is relatively well known and reaches out to the approver for advice or guidance, perhaps on how best to guide the start-up financially. This connection not only results in amazing advice and guidance but also can be the beginning of an excellent business deal.

This all seems so obvious to me, but our experience at TAG suggests that many start-ups do not take the time for this essential task: Learn the interests of your target customers, whether champion or approver, and engage based on these interests. This is human interaction 101.

Buyer Background

A second tribal trait for buyers is a common background, and this is often based on region or culture, both of which are powerful, such as a Portuguese founder selling to a buyer of Portuguese background. The common background could also be corporate, as with a former IBM employee selling to a colleague who had also been at IBM. And it could also be domain-specific, such as an energy industry expert selling to an energy industry veteran.

Perhaps the most often encountered example of common background involves the military. Just about every successful military sales engagement that I have ever seen in my four decades of work involved some sort of military background on the part of the seller. This works best with a personal connection, but it can also be indirect. My dad, for example, worked for three decades for the U.S. Army, and I proudly reference this fact with buyers from that segment.

Common backgrounds between start-ups and their target customers—including both champions and approvers—create an environment of mutual trust. For any start-up, this development of trust is one of the great hurdles, especially for larger buyers who might be concerned with the viability of the new company. Shared backgrounds can lessen the intensity of the business risk taken by the buyer in dealing with your early-stage company.

Your discussions, interactions, and other engagements with customers should be tailored to their background, including, of course, technical backgrounds. If your solution goes deep into a specific domain, such as finance, accounting, software, or manufacturing, then you absolutely must consider the backgrounds of the individuals you are targeting. Roughly speaking, champions tend to have domain-specific backgrounds, and approvers do not.

Just about every start-up we encounter has something called a standard deck. This involves those dreaded PowerPoint charts developed by the marketing team in approved fonts and colors. This deck is usually stipulated for use on all customer presentations. With a standard deck, sometimes you'll be right (broken clocks are correct twice per day), but on many, many occasions, you will strike the wrong tone.

For example, security companies trying to drive influence through TAG to their target customers often pitch their ideas to me. I am hardly a wallflower, with my large social media presence and reasonably large footprint on the internet. Despite that, I can't tell you how many start-ups fill the first fifteen minutes with me with offers of tutorial guidance on an industry I helped to invent. Their ignorance reflects a lack of preparation.

Here is my advice regarding backgrounds: First, engage with buyers with detailed attention to their backgrounds. Try to include team members in the sales life cycle who share a similar background to buyers. Second, please get rid of the standard deck. Always tailor your pitch to the backgrounds of the individuals you are connecting with. (We will discuss how to determine these backgrounds later in this chapter.)

Buyer Aspirations

The third element of the tribe involves aspirations, the personal goals, hopes, and dreams of the buying individual, whether champion or approver. Great sales teams have always understood how critical it is to understand the aspirations of their buyers because, if the sales team can help them achieve their dreams, it will always make the sale. In B2B environments, the aspirations of buyers are often wrapped up in career goals at their company.

Focusing on aspirations allows your success selling to become entwined with the success of your customer. When an individual becomes the internal champion for your product, for example, then they have essentially staked their reputation on you. If you succeed in delivering value, then you should have a customer for life.

Here is a B2B example: Suppose that you are connecting with a potential champion who is brand new to their job. Perhaps they are also brand new to the industry and the entire area in which your team focuses. Imagine the connection that emerges if you approach the champion and offer to include private coaching, specialized training, and customized help whenever something might demand some clarity. The result would be amazing.

I also like the idea, whenever possible, of requesting that approvers join your advisory board (and, of course, you should have one). From an aspirational perspective, 100 percent of executives view board work as part of their future career planning. If you can offer a means for developing some board expertise, then you are directly tapping into a major element of their personal career aspiration. Even if they are not approved to join, they will remember the gesture.

Buyer Culture

The fourth and perhaps most important element of the tribe is culture, which refers to common habits, behaviors, beliefs, and expectations held by members of the tribe. Culture can involve common patterns of speech, manners of dress, and belief system tendencies, and regional considerations related to country, family, and even sports or hobbies. Tribes take these traits seriously, so it is wise not to ignore them.

For example, the soldier in every country encounters a norm for military tribe members that involves honor, duty, integrity, and courage. When selling to this tribe, you must decide if these traits are consistent with your own. If they are, then you will have great success with this tribe. But if they are not, then you cannot fake these belief systems. You will need to target your selling toward belief systems and cultures consistent with your own.

The software development community exhibits a unique culture that is often hard to understand unless you are part of it. Think about the concept of working for many hours without pay on an open-source software project, not because you want to increase your bank balance but because you want to advance your profession. This is an amazing trait, and if you cannot understand it, then you cannot sell to it.

You will note, I hope, that we are not talking about the toxic culture-war issues that permeate so many societies. I've lectured at length, for example, about the need for different groups across the United States to come together. Culture wars are not appropriate for start-ups, and we coach our founders not to go near these issues.

If you do find that team members are using politics or other divisive issues as the basis for selling, then we recommend that you put a stop to this practice. In the short term, you might connect with someone aligned with your beliefs inside some balkanized group. In the long term, the tribal traits that really matter are ones that do not divide people but rather celebrate positive belief systems that drive common purpose.

CYBERSECURITY EXAMPLE: TRIBES OF BUYERS

Readers who are familiar with the cybersecurity industry will understand that this discipline is relatively new and that the typical buyer is tough to characterize—unlike doctors, lawyers, or marines. Cybersecurity professionals, especially as they break off into champions and approvers, come from a wide variety of backgrounds, including information technology (IT), finance, software, and so on.

The tendencies and traits that define the various tribes in cybersecurity do not separate perfectly into groups of champions and approvers, as one might expect in most engineering fields. But there is a correlation. The champions tend to have interests in malware signatures, network protocols, security risk equations, and so on. Approvers, as in most fields, tend to have more interest in business and finance.

You can find other interesting traits in this industry. Regarding culture, there are two distinct cultural approaches to cybersecurity. The first is the offensive culture, which is exhibited by hackers. If you attend a hacker conference, you will meet people wearing black tee-shirts and grumbling endlessly about the annoying influence of government.

The defensive culture, in contrast, is exhibited by enterprise security teams and IT security executives. If you meet these folks, their culture is more corporate, and their conferences are conventional, vendor-dominated events with talks, speeches, dinners, and free merchandise.

Regarding aspirations, there is also a clear divide within the cybersecurity community, aligned with the offensive and defensive cultures. Offensive-minded hackers want the approval of their community. They spend day and night working for no reason other than to become recognized by people they admire. Sellers should be looking for this trait, even in traditional companies such as banks or government agencies.

Defensive-minded practitioners aspire more to the hefty salaries paid to CISOs. Start-ups who sell to this tribe must be focused on this career aspiration to understand that buyer. It is about as different from the hacker aspiration as one can imagine.

Founders selling into a specific area such as cybersecurity must become experts in identifying, understanding, and targeting specific tribes within their target buying community. It takes some skill to make this determination, but our taxonomy of common interest, background, aspirations, and culture should serve as a North Star in making this absolutely essential determination for your start-up team.

TRIBAL SELLING CASE STUDY: VMWARE

As we have shown with case studies on Apple, Google, and other large companies, start-ups can often learn from the approaches taken by larger organizations—and VMware is an excellent example. Recently acquired by Broadcom, VMware is itself an enormous entity that TAG has worked with for years. It does a wonderful job tailoring its solutions to individual tribes. Let's spend some time on VMware's approach.

VMware sells two types of solutions. First, it sells software to data center operators, usually larger entities who are not often described as using the cloud because they are, in essence, the cloud. These operators run massive infrastructure that must be simplified and streamlined to support modern applications such as AI and next-generation operations technology (e.g., robotic manufacturing).

Second, VMware also sells to enterprise teams who are completely integrated into a cloud-based hybrid environment. These are bread-and-butter organizations that love how VMware helps them virtualize their operation. By "virtualize," we mean that VMware helps turn tangible hardware systems into software (such as how your iPhone makes calculator software, where previously it was a physical device).

As you might expect, the marketing collateral, sales processes, and support infrastructure for these different buyers have to be tailored to their specific needs. The approach taken by VMware, and frankly many other large companies, is to organize each buyer into something called segments. This is marketing 101—namely, segmenting your customer base. Most start-ups, however, do not perform this task well.

In contrast, we've watch VMware expertly take its underlying base of capability related to its virtualization technology and then instantiate different interpretations, examples, and illustrations for its various segments. I know this firsthand because I have helped them do this—and they are world-class at it. They never waver from a common technology base, but they understand that different segments have different needs.

For start-ups, this should be the approach taken, although the extent to which it must be done might be more limited. As a massive organization, VMware touches virtually every type of buying tribe imaginable. This might explain why it has gone to such lengths to ensure a tailored message for each group. The teams at AT&T and M&T Bank, during my periods of service there, were also good at understanding their customer segments.

The obligation for your start-up founding team is that you must take the time to segment your customer base. Remember that they are buying because of your belief system, innovations, and disruptions. Thus, you must understand their psyche, perhaps even more than a larger entity that can sell to mass markets based on product features.

TRIBAL SELLING CASE STUDY: SOLARWINDS

In 2020, Russian hackers successfully breached the software of an IT management vendor called SolarWinds. This was a consequential attack because many companies used the compromised utility across their enterprise network. Government agencies were hit especially hard with the breach because the hackers gained access to the data, networks, and systems of any user who had deployed SolarWinds.

The incident quickly became a nightmare for the entire industry, and the press covered the story and analyzed how various companies and agencies were patching and updating their SolarWinds software. Into this situation entered a new SolarWinds CEO, Sudhakar Ramakrishna. I knew Ramakrishna from his prior work at a cybersecurity company called Pulse Secure, which had been a TAG customer.

Given our understanding at TAG of his wonderful executive capability, we were not surprised at how expertly this new CEO dealt with the public relations challenges at his new company. He was even kind enough to spend time with my New York University graduate students explaining how he addressed his tough situation. It was an impressive lesson in explaining clearly and honestly what happened and what was being done.

SolarWinds is an interesting case study in dealing with tribes because it sells its platform to two different, often budget-competing groups—namely, the team running IT operations and the team running IT security. The first group must ensure that users have the right IT tools and services for their day-to-day work, and the second group must ensure that sufficient controls are in place to prevent or mitigate anything that compromises security.

The first group is incentivized to say yes to all IT requests, while the other is motivated to say no for reasons related to security. And it does not help that senior leadership often pits the groups against each other when it comes to budget. Situations thus emerge where IT might like to buy something that security does not recommend, but if IT controls the budget, it can move forward anyway.

As a result, the company must clearly differentiate its sales, support, and posthacking incident messaging between the two groups. When talking to IT operations teams, SolarWinds must provide guidance on how they enable cloud services, software-as-a-service (SaaS) applications, mobile platforms, web applications, advanced networking, and other capabilities. We watched as the company explained the implications of the hack on these areas of IT.

But when dealing with security teams, SolarWinds must not only emphasize its protection capabilities but also explain how it has taken steps to avoid another nation-state hacking situation. It's a difficult tightrope, and Ramakrishna has the experience and background to speak confidently and expertly with both types of buying tribes. It was an excellent lesson for those of us watching in how to message to two different buying groups.

USING LINKEDIN TO IDENTIFY TRIBES

We have referred to the sales process throughout these beginning chapters, but it makes sense to offer a word or two about an important component of that process—namely, the sales pitch. (The topic is also addressed in detail later in the book.) The sales pitch is the time, often virtually, when the sales team tells their story to a customer. We acknowledge that a sales discussion is a better approach than a sales pitch, but this is not an important distinction for now.

Before you engage in any sales pitch, you must take the time to determine exactly who you will be pitching to. This might be an individual, a group, or some other combination of folks you might or might not know. Even emails sent to prospects are part of the sales pitch, so research into the tribal traits of someone you are emailing is highly recommended.

You may use a customer relationship management (CRM) tool such as HubSpot or Salesforce to blast out thousands of spam emails to target customers. And I fully understand that you probably view yourself as too busy to research the targets. But if you want to improve the response rate from one in a thousand to one in a hundred, then you will have to take the time to research contacts.

This is an important enough point for repeat: If you are too busy to research contacts, then you are too busy to be successful at sales.

In our experience working with start-ups, we have found that LinkedIn is the most effective means for determining the tribe of a target buyer. This social network has become the de facto database of timely and up-to-date information on almost every businessperson on the globe. It is a treasure trove of data about literally every B2B decision maker. And it can also help with B2C research as you work through the tribes of buyers for consumer offerings.

It is also vital for start-up team members to maintain their own LinkedIn presence by taking full advantage of the platform within the terms and conditions of acceptable use, of course. When you are planning a pitch to a group, review the individuals who will be present either in person or virtually and develop a dossier for each that is focused on information that helps to identify their tribe. It's not a hard process.

This is not some inappropriate means for categorizing or dividing people; rather, it is a reasonable and effective approach to learn from public sources about the people to whom you are trying to sell. Too many start-ups skip this step, and this is unfortunate because the data is so readily available.

Commit to this now: You will no longer do any sales pitch or discussion without first carefully determining the tribe of your sales target.

EXAMPLE CUSTOMER PROFILE: PAMELA DOE

To illustrate how a social media profile can be used to guide an accurate determination of a target customer's tribal traits, let's create a hypothetical person named Pamela Doe. We'll assume that you run a start-up company that sells a novel AI-based software product that scans a customer's marketing materials to remove any references that might come from fake news or other misinformation on the internet.

Let's assume that you recently held a webinar with your top technical person explaining how your solution uses marketing material from the internet as training data. The software then cross-references the training material with any reports of fakes news. After the webinar, you receive a request from someone named Pamela Doe requesting more information on the platform. The customer suggests a Zoom session.

My experience is that most of these leads will go to a salesperson (call her Alison) in the start-up supported by someone in the title of sales engineer (call him Adam). They are handed the lead and told to set up a call, which they do. On the day of the briefing, Alison and Adam have five briefings that they fit between breaks, lunch, and a few internal meetings. Alison and Adam are busy, but they work well together.

The Zoom call is started by Alison at the planned time, and they see that Pamela is already in the waiting room. Alison holds off on adding the customer so that she and Adam can remember what this call is all about. They check email and conclude that this is a cold call from a webinar and that the customer probably doesn't know much about the company. Everything seems normal, and Alison adds the customer to the call.

When the customer's face appears on screen, Alison gets started: "I'm so sorry we kept you waiting, Pam. We are just so busy jumping from one customer to another. It's so crazy here." The customer responds that she prefers to be called Pamela, to which Alison apologizes. After sharing pleasantries about the weather, Alison offers to share information about the company and platform. Pamela nods in agreement.

Alison then fires up a presentation that explains the broad challenges of modern marketing professionals. It is tutorial information because Alison has been told that most prospects don't know the first thing about marketing. This is the tenth time Alison has done this in the last two days. She goes through the material and barely notices that the customer has gone off video during her discussion.

In a smooth transition, Alison hands it over to Adam who then goes through a demonstration of the platform. He clicks here and there and shows that the platform can do this and that. It's all

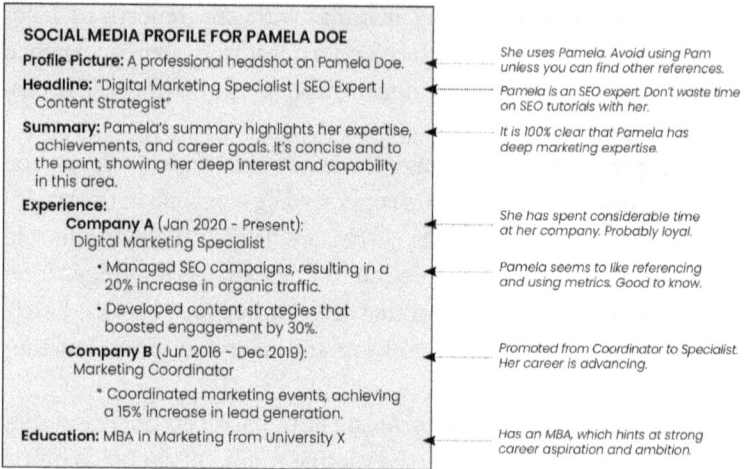

SOCIAL MEDIA PROFILE FOR PAMELA DOE

Profile Picture: A professional headshot on Pamela Doe. — *She uses Pamela. Avoid using Pam unless you can find other references.*

Headline: "Digital Marketing Specialist | SEO Expert | Content Strategist" — *Pamela is an SEO expert. Don't waste time on SEO tutorials with her.*

Summary: Pamela's summary highlights her expertise, achievements, and career goals. It's concise and to the point, showing her deep interest and capability in this area. — *It is 100% clear that Pamela has deep marketing expertise.*

Experience:
    Company A (Jan 2020 - Present): Digital Marketing Specialist — *She has spent considerable time at her company. Probably loyal.*
        • Managed SEO campaigns, resulting in a 20% increase in organic traffic. — *Pamela seems to like referencing and using metrics. Good to know.*
        • Developed content strategies that boosted engagement by 30%.
    Company B (Jun 2016 - Dec 2019): Marketing Coordinator — *Promoted from Coordinator to Specialist. Her career is advancing.*
        * Coordinated marketing events, achieving a 15% increase in lead generation.

Education: MBA in Marketing from University X — *Has an MBA, which hints at strong career aspiration and ambition.*

Figure 3.2 Social media profile for fictitious customer, Pamela Doe

pretty mechanical. When Adam is done, he leaves two minutes for any questions from Pamela. She comes back on camera and politely thanks them, explaining that she needs to get to another meeting.

In our example, we assumed that Pamela knew little about marketing or the platform. But how do we know this? Alison and Adam certainly did not check, and they could have easily gotten information about Pamela from her social media profile. Figure 3.2 shows some information that perhaps Alison and Adam would have found had they taken five minutes to research the customer.

From Pamela's profile, they would have learned that her proper name was Pamela (and it is such a gaffe that Alison started the discussion with an apology about getting the customer's name wrong). Next, they would have determined that the entire front end of the discussion could have been skipped because Pamela knows more about marketing and related topics than Alison or Adam combined.

By skipping the front end, they could have asked Pamela about her actual interests, perhaps even skipping the demo. The point is that, without taking the time to learn that Pamela is a marketing expert with an MBA, she is loyal to her firm, and she has an advancing career and deep expertise in her discipline, Alison and Adam are basically throwing crap at the wall. And they will wonder afterward why Pamela did not bother following up.

TAILORING THE PITCH TO THE TRIBE

What, you might ask, is one to do when armed with this information about the specific tribe to which one or more target buyers belong? Should the sales pitch or other aspect of a sales engagement be tailored to some stereotype of that tribe? As we showed with the example above, tailoring to a stereotype is correct. And no, identifying a person as technical and assuming they might like to learn more about how a product works is not stereotyping. It is showing respect for a customer.

Keep in mind that when you spend time learning the tribals traits of those you are pitching to, your preparation makes their time with you more interesting, and you minimize any time wasted with them on information, charts, or other material that they are likely to find redundant or unimportant. This is a key point, and it is ignored for two reasons: It takes time, and it is just plain hard work.

Let's remind ourselves again of how tailoring is done best. First, you should not be changing your belief system or reason for being. The founding story of your start-up, for example, should not change, and it should be commonly and consistently reinforced across all the various tribes to which you are pitching. This is good news because it helps to tie together your messaging with a common foundational base.

Once you begin to identify the interests, backgrounds, aspirations, and cultures of the individuals or groups to which you are hoping to sell, that is where you begin to tailor the messaging. You will make decisions, for example, about whether to highlight and emphasize your growth story, your high-level solution architecture, or the lowest-level details of your implementation.

We acknowledge that sometimes you will have a hodgepodge of different tribal traits coming together, for example, at a large briefing with a potential client. This simply demands that you work to include something for everyone and to offer separate sessions or breakout discussions with the various subgroups. This is not that complicated, but we see start-ups every day treat their customer in a monolithic manner. This is not the best approach.

If you want to truly connect with your buyer, then learn their tribal traits and tailor your message to their interests. This is good business, and it is a show of respect for your customer.

PART TWO

ENLIGHTENMENT

4

WHO ARE YOUR COMPETITORS?

When I ask start-ups about their competitors, the most popular answer by far is that they don't have any competition. "We are the only ones who do what we do" is the standard response from the founder or chief marketing officer. And when I hear this, I just pause, sigh, and plunge into an explanation of the pitfalls of the so-called category of one—even when you are an early start-up. This is true for both business-to-business (B2B) and business-to-consumer (B2C) companies.

Rather than seek to be in a category of one, I believe that the best positioning for any start-up offering is a new take on something familiar. When I see that, I bump up my enthusiasm for the company tenfold.

No founder wants to lose business to a competitor, but this is a small price to pay for not having to justify to buyers why you are the only one doing what you do. Many corporate procurement teams do not even allow purchase of a product from a start-up unless the internal sponsor can list at least two or three viable options to compare pricing, servicing, and value.

I understand that you want to tell prospects that you are inventing the future in a manner that no one else has conceived. We are not suggesting that you avoid being creative and different—you must be both. But if your objective is to sell, then you need competition, if only to demonstrate that there is an actual market need for what you do.

Another popular answer from start-ups when they are asked about competition is to respond without any mention of the most obvious competitor. This would be like a new fast-food hamburger restaurant not listing McDonalds as a competitor. When I push back, however, the founder responds almost inevitably with something along the lines of: "McDonalds? No, we almost never see them in the fast-food hamburger market."

Ignoring the elephant-in-the-room competitor is ill advised. Founders can try to believe that their top competitor doesn't exist, but you can be certain that buyers will not believe it. My advice has been consistent in this regard: The time spent trying to understand your real competition is generally an excellent investment, one that will help you gain deeper insights into your market and create better means for improving your product.

ASYMMETRIC VERSUS SYMMETRIC COMPETITION

Because start-ups are almost always smaller than more established companies, a situation often emerges where a new company founder is targeting a much larger competitor. Venture capital can distort this picture somewhat, but the size differential is usually true. When this occurs, buyers may well enjoy the David-versus-Goliath situation where the young, scrappy start-up is on a mission to slay the large, greedy monster.

As suggested in the preface, my own company follows this playbook with Gartner and the similar analyst firm, Forrester, both much larger than TAG. We have noticed shortcomings in the customer satisfaction for both firms (you are welcome to review your own experience or speak with other buyers of their services). We never ran any formal research, but significant anecdotal experience suggests that our slay-the-dragon mission against Gartner works well.

This situation is referred to as asymmetric competition. When a start-up engages in this type of business warfare, several approaches are recommended. First, it is essential that the start-up emphasizes their mission and invites customers to join them on the journey. I really like those two words in this context: "mission" and "journey." They are the primary keys to unlock successful competition with a larger competitor.

An additional visceral weapon that can be used in the asymmetric fight against a larger competitor involves your purpose. Your mission to slay the dragon allows your customers to share in your goals and objectives. Don't discount the fun buyers have in watching an underdog succeed. Use this to your advantage if you can. Use the leverage to help you bring customers in line with your purpose. They will help you reach the chasm.

CASE STUDY: APPLE VERSUS IBM

Steve Jobs understood how to connect with buyers at a much deeper level than product features. We referenced earlier his idea that Apple would be focused on challenging the status quo and that customers who believed similarly should join the Apple revolution. This belief system, in my estimation, is why the company is worth trillions today.

We often forget that Apple was once a tiny company and when Jobs was just beginning as a founder, he followed the David-and-Goliath playbook perfectly. For him, IBM served as his large dragon to be slayed, and he went after IBM at every opportunity during the early days of Apple.

I've tried to follow this symbolism at TAG with cartoons. Several years ago, I started a new cartoon series called Charlie CISO, which has become popular in the technology nerd sector. Each week, the great illustrator Rich Powell and I collaborate on a new one-panel *New Yorker*–style cartoon or a three-panel Dilbert-style cartoon narrative that makes a case (we hope humorously) about something related to TAG's business. You should have no trouble finding our cartoons on the internet, including on LinkedIn.

We use the series to poke fun at anything in sight, from the U.S. federal government to Israeli start-up founders—and to poke fun at Gartner. One cartoon shows two bums sitting on the sidewalk, and one says to the other: "I probably shouldn't have listened to Gartner." Another shows two cars waiting at a light. One car is a souped-up sports car, and the license plate says, "TAG;" the other is a broken-down jalopy, and its license plate says, "Gartner."

Asymmetric competition provides the opportunity, as you've seen with both early Apple and current TAG, for start-ups to invite their customers to join the fun slaying the big dragon.

DIRECT COMPETITION

Start-ups must also deal with the problem of direct competition. To the horror of most founders, many start-ups find competing offers from other start-ups that include a similar product being sold to similar customers from a similar founding team. In cybersecurity, for example, I run into Israeli founders from Unit 8200 starting new companies based on their military experience and bumping up against literally dozens of mirror entities doing essentially the same thing.

In my experience, this is usually the most uncomfortable type of competitor for start-up founders and marketing teams to acknowledge when they are asked about it. Such discomfort is usually the wrong emotion for start-up leaders because competing entities can be useful in creating a category. Later in the book, in chapter 7, we'll provide guidance on how to deal with industry analysts, but it might be helpful to provide a preliminary glance here.

The general idea is that, by combining several competitors into a logical group, analysts can advise clients about some general capability associated with a given group of vendors and to then instantiate and even rate and rank the vendors in that group with respect to some defined set of comparison criteria. As one might expect, this helps buyers organize their thinking as well as plan for and obtain budget.

It should be obvious that if only one start-up is working in a given area, then analysts and buyers will have trouble conceptualizing whether that start-up is addressing something sufficiently urgent and relevant. A common joke is that when you are the only one working in an area, then there might be a good reason for that. If several start-ups are doing similar work, however, this is evidence that value is being created and buyers should pay attention.

The category creation, if done properly, will be driven by real problems faced by customers. Think of electric vehicle (EV) charging infrastructure, for example. Potential and current EV drivers lament the availability of easy-to-find charging stations; as companies emerge to solve this problem, a category is created based on such activity.

Start-ups might also be created based on categories that are more aspirational. Quantum computing, for example, is an area where we see many new start-ups that lack clarity on the actual market. Aspirational development without clarity of the category can be risky and fragile, but this is the conundrum of innovation.

Whether you are dealing with direct or indirect competition, the best start-ups always keep their eye on developing solutions that can be described as a new take on something familiar.

STRATEGIES FOR DIRECT COMPETITION

Two strategies work well for start-ups dealing with direct competition. First, your start-up must have a unique statement of purpose. If you develop your statement of purpose properly, then it will, by definition, be different from your direct competition. This allows you to draw attention away from a similar product or service and more toward the unique belief systems and "why" statements that are personal to your founding team and adopted across your company.

Second, you should follow a strategy that might seem counterintuitive: Celebrate your direct competition. Point out their strengths. Reference them as partners in crime in your journey to disrupt the larger, asymmetric competition. Position your team and that of your nearest direct competitor as two small wolves dealing with a nasty leopard. Point out to prosects that you are going after the leopard and not the other gazelle.

Keep in mind the image of the original black-and-white film Miracle of 34th Street where Santa Claus advised Macy's customers to visit Gimbel's if they had a better product. That is a good metaphor, in our opinion, for dealing with direct competition. Save the direct warfare for when you cross the chasm because your near-term goal is to capture innovators and early adopters. You are not ready yet to capture a majority of customers.

In summary, when you must deal with direct competition, focus on your purpose and celebrate your direct competitors. This strategy will endear you to early clients and will position you for direct warfare when you eventually grow large enough to reach the chasm.

CASE STUDY: CROWDSTRIKE VERSUS CYLANCE

The idea that you want competition should be clear by now. This does not imply, however, that you and your direct competitors will turn out in the same manner. Let's take the case of two prominent cybersecurity companies: CrowdStrike and Cylance. Some of you will no doubt recognize the name CrowdStrike from their massive outage on Windows system in 2024.

The story starts for me back in the early 2000s when I first heard of an interesting start-up company called Foundstone. Around that time, I had been using in my work at AT&T an IBM tool to scan the emerging perimeter network edge that was so common for companies at that time. The IBM solution worked fine, but I was never quite satisfied with its output.

I had been reading a book at the time called *Hacking Exposed*, which I think is in its fifth edition today. It was basically a compendium of hacks—and I noticed that two of their authors, Stu McClure and George Kurtz, were also now running a scanning company called Foundstone. "This is cool," I remember thinking. "A start-up based on research in a book."

After my team reviewed the scanning tool from this start-up, we made the decision to replace IBM's tool with the scanner from Foundstone, which I suspect was helpful to this brand-new company. Thus began my awareness of these two fine entrepreneurs and their work supporting enterprise security teams. You can probably guess that I was both the champion and approver on this one.

The Foundstone company was eventually sold to McAfee for $86 million in 2004. In the mid to late 2010s, however, I was approached by both McClure and Kurtz on sales calls, and they each told me about their new companies—Cylance (McClure) and CrowdStrike (Kurtz), and I'll be darned if their stories didn't sound somewhat similar. The technical details were different, but the founding purposes seemed to rhyme.

Cylance was perhaps a bit more into the AI angle, and Crowd-Strike more into the forensics and incident response approach. But like the "what" statements for most start-ups, the functional characteristics of the offerings evolved. Over time, both companies seemed to move squarely into end-point protection, and these two friends became competitors. (I spent money with both—and I especially liked Cylance's AI solution, but that's another story).

Soon after both companies were on their way, I started TAG, and both McClure and Kurtz became early customers. They each signed up for content and advisory services, so I got an early glimpse into the direction that each of these iconic founders was headed. One thing you will learn in chapter 7 is that analyst firms do work with competing entities in much the same way as movie critics rate movies from competing production houses.

McClure sold his company to Blackberry for a staggering $1.4 billion in 2019. I believe Blackberry should have begged the Cylance founder to become its CEO, but no one at Blackberry asked for my opinion. McClure left Blackberry just months after the acquisition and is now running a new start-up called Qwiet (a TAG customer) that does AI for software.

As for CrowdStrike, Kurtz evolved his solution toward protection of laptops, PCs, and other user devices—and I hope our early advisory work was helpful to the company in this regard. Today, Crowd-Strike is a public company with over $2 billion in revenue and over seven hundred employees. They are generally regarded as one of the most successful cybersecurity firms in the world, used often as a metaphor for other companies (e.g., "We hope to be the CrowdStrike of this-or-that").

We referenced the CrowdStrike outage in 2024 that caused considerable damage to users. This type of incident often occurs with any start-up that races across the chasm quickly. This is not the start-up's fault. Success breeds growth. Now, CrowdStrike will need to install a new set of business controls, including probably an expanded bureaucracy, because they have shifted from start-up to critical infrastructure in just a few years.

But perhaps more consistent with our story is that I fundamentally believe that both Cylance and CrowdStrike were made better by the direct competition. Had either company been couched as some category-of-one innovator doing work no one on the planet could have ever conceived, then I think their stories would have been quite different—and probably nowhere near as positive.

FEATURE COMPARISON CHARTS

I have never run into a start-up or investor that, when asking for a competitive landscape review, is not actually asking for a detailed comparison of features. You have probably seen the results of these comparisons, which are usually developed in a *Consumer Reports*–style chart with all the competing products along the side as rows and all the presumably relevant features in the various products along the top as columns.

The reviewer (which is often our team at TAG, but many, many others do this type of analysis as well) will then provide some sort of scoring of whether the product from ACME provides more or less coverage than the product from Consolidated, Amalgamated, and so on. It's a daunting exercise because making these determinations is difficult, and they must be made as a snapshot in time. And everyone knows that product features change quickly.

Such comparisons generally result in one of two situations. If the comparison is stacked to depict the requesting entity (also known as the paying client) as being superior to all others, then everyone gets a nice near-term hit of dopamine, so to speak. The founders are happy, the investors are happy, and the analyst is paid—not only for the analysis but usually for many subsequent analyses. These types of comparisons usually result in a chart like the one shown in figure 4.1.

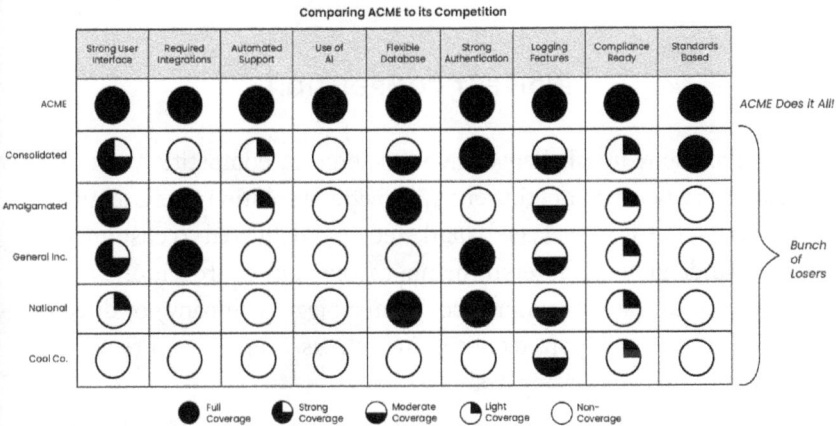

Figure 4.1 Sample start-up feature comparison chart

If the comparison shows deep challenges in terms of features, however, then there is often some real friction that emerges. We have found that this occurs when small companies are compared with larger entities that have more feature-rich platforms. For your own start-up, we recommend that you resist the urge to do this type of work, but we are 100 percent certain that your investors will not let you avoid this step.

In chapter 7 we will discuss how you deal with analysts, which will inevitably bring up the challenge of quadrants, waves, and ratings. These are intended to be done in an unbiased manner, but this is often not the case. When we get to that discussion, we'll help you deal with the challenge of interpreting a bad (or good) rating from a presumably independent external analyst firm.

If you decide to commission a feature comparison as part of your competitive analysis, then please do not take the result too seriously—whether good or bad. The comparison will change, and we've already told you throughout this book that your belief system is ten times more important in attracting disruptors and innovators then whether your interface has more widgets than a competitor does.

INDIRECT COMPETITION

Another start-up challenge involves indirect competition, which emerges when a competing entity provides a solution that is similar to yours, but it is packaged, marketed, and delivered to customers in a fundamentally different manner from your approach. Indirect competition can be asymmetric (from a bigger company) or direct (from a comparably sized entity). In both cases, however, it requires attention to avoid losing deals.

One example is an environmental, social, and governance (ESG) consulting start-up made up of experts offering insights to business leaders. Direct competition would come from similarly small start-ups comprised of experts with similar capabilities. Indirect competition would involve a large consulting firms providing broad consultation that could include ESG as part of a broader advisory relationship.

To compete in this scenario, the start-up must first be nimble, which implies the ability to shift focus quickly and easily based on interactions with the client. If the goals of the work require an adjustment, larger entities will have to resort to the master service agreement, perhaps even with lawyers. But smaller start-ups can emphasize their willingness to adjust on the fly, and customers will like this immensely.

Start-ups can also offer surgically targeted capability. I come from a large business environment where we had to scale solutions to every type of business one could imagine. People would ask me which of the Fortune 500 companies I supported during my time in telecommunications, and the answer was all of them. This had the advantage of offering broad visibility into the general needs of all businesses.

But such broad coverage precluded our ability to innovate as rapidly as a start-up. We had to develop standard solutions that would scale, and this required adherence to stable offers. Every large business knows that start-ups can introduce more innovative approaches more quickly because their risk tolerance is so much lower. As my colleague at TAG Dave Neuman would put it: This is the superpower of a start-up.

When you see a solution comparable to your own that is embedded into something broader that is delivered by an organization that you would normally not consider competition, you should focus on two things: (1) Offer the option for nimble support that can be adjusted as needed, and (2) provide surgically innovative solutions that can enjoy the luxury of not having to be sufficiently broad to support every possible customer. That is, you can focus on your customer.

CASE STUDY: TAG VERSUS GARTNER

At TAG, we compete asymmetrically and indirectly with Gartner. They are one thousand times larger than our company. We are growing, but we are still a galaxy away from their billions in revenue. While our team comes from backgrounds in which we dealt with revenue orders of magnitude higher than Gartner, we have now thrust ourselves into the position of being the smaller disrupting challenger with a tiny percentage of market share.

This begs a strategy that focuses on the themes mentioned above—being nimble and innovative. But it has also allowed us to develop marketing themes to differentiate ourselves based on experience. Despite Gartner's size, the actual analyst assigned to a business customer from Gartner, in the area of cybersecurity, will have at least a decade or more less experience than an analyst from our team at TAG (we checked and did the math).

We have noticed that this experience theme plays not only with customers but also with the mainstream media. *Fast Company* recently noticed what we were doing and decided to do a piece on our company. I was delighted because I'd been a reader of that magazine for so long, and when I started TAG, I told my wife that one of my goals was to be featured in their publication. This was a bucket item to check.

To my surprise, as I got into the discussion with the interviewer from *Fast Company*, it became clear that she was particularly interested in my experience and also my age. What eventually popped out was a 2022 piece in their magazine entitled: "The Secret of My Success as an Entrepreneur: I'm 60." While it would be nice to be twenty years younger, you are who you are—and we've noticed that our clients like this, too.

Entrepreneur magazine also reinforced this theme with an interview piece on our company that had a much better title: "How This Entrepreneur Seeks to Disrupt Traditional Cybersecurity Research." But if you read the narrative, our years of experience remain a major theme. If you are a start-up company competing with a massive entity, then find that unique strength the bigger company cannot match and go with it.

COMPETING PROMOTIONAL APPROACHES

Another type of indirect competition that I've seen in my work emerges when two start-ups with similar products decide to promote their solutions in completely different ways. This is often fascinating to watch because their products can have more or less the same capability, but the means by which the products are marketed, advertised, promoted, and even delivered can be quite different.

One scenario involves a start-up using a broad, expansive message delivered as loudly as possible. This is the shout-from-the-mountaintop approach, and the team uses marketing budget to proclaim their story in every manner possible. I remember stepping into the airport in San Francisco several years ago and seeing a floor-to-ceiling mural of Stuart McClure from Cylance on the wall. That is a loud message.

In contrast, a competing start-up might decide on a quieter and more personalized message delivered in a less prominent, word-of-mouth setting. You might think this to be a more passive approach, but we have watched companies like McKinsey and Bain do this effectively. You rarely see them use blaring ads. Instead, they try to allow their work to speak for itself and to move from one client to another without big media campaigns.

There is nothing right or wrong with either approach, and we usually recommend that a start-up try to determine which works better—and then go all in on that approach. It is worth pointing out that B2C start-ups usually focus on the more broad, expansive option, trying to use social media, conference booths, direct email campaigns, Google ads, and other options to get noticed. TAG often assists with content in this regard.

The mission for the early-stage start-up is to attract innovator and early adopter customers, however, and we've been clear that this is based on shared beliefs. Because belief systems are so personal, one might wonder if the shout-from-the-billboard approach is always best. A larger firm that has already crossed the chasm will almost certainly have to be loud in its promotion (McKinsey and Bain are exceptions).

At some point in your early stage, you will have to decide which of the two approaches works best. And before deciding to use both, recognize that in some disciplines such as security, the quiet approach is a good metaphor for the confidentiality and obscurity that are often indicative of the best protection approaches. Our advice is to decide on one approach—and then go all in.

CASE STUDY: MCAFEE VERSUS PCMATIC

The McAfee company was created in 1987 by a highly controversial person named John McAfee. You can search his story on the internet, but do so without the kids because you'll find videos of him cavorting with strippers, claiming to have been nabbed by some cartel, and doing of lot of other crazy stuff.

McAfee became a TAG client around the time that I began the company, and it was one of our largest billing customers for several years. From the beginning, McAfee spent considerable money on its product, it focused on marketing, and it gave great support to customers. It was an iconic company that had the best (in my opinion) approach to stopping malware on end-point PCs and servers. I used their product for over a decade.

Hacking approaches eventually changed, however, and the company struggled to find its footing. It is now folded into a new company called Trellix that delivers an excellent product, albeit without the iconic McAfee brand. It's a bittersweet story because McAfee had always stressed technical excellence, and today, most practitioners would view the brand as being largely defunct. They promoted according to the playbook, and it eventually failed.

In massive contrast stands an unusual antimalware company called PCMatic. I first noticed this company on television where they were running advertisements showing their company staff playing security songs as a rock band, including the founder on guitar. The music was so bad, and the commercials were so annoying that it was just impossible to flip the channel, sort of like a bad train wreck.

Search the internet and you can watch these commercials, but please do not blame me when you hum the bad tunes all day, which I suppose is the point. I called their CEO a couple of years ago hoping to learn more about the company, and I was directed to their marketing team, which was kind enough to brief me on its solution and business approach on two occasions.

While it never became a TAG client, I learned this: PCMatic spends a lot of money on TV commercials, and they are growing like crazy. Some of their schtick is a tad over the top for me, including the nationalistic claims about being the only U.S. company doing cybersecurity. Their commercials target a demographic (mostly older folks watching the conservative political channels) who probably do not care about the product and but do care about the message.

I researched the collective technical capability of the PCMatic product and found the solution to include mostly me-too whitelisting and a less than stellar technical support staff, some of whom appeared to move from jobs such as managing retail stores to PCMatic positions as malware analysts. But the proof is in the pudding, so to speak. They sell product, and lots of it.

It is just so interesting to me that McAfee, with its amazing technical capability, textbook promotion, and excellent customer support, eventually struggled and is now basically defunct. PCMatic, with its weaker technology and less-than-stellar staff, but with all those crazy TV commercials pitching to senior citizens, has grown. Business success is not always so easy to predict.

BUDGET COMPETITION

The next type of competition involves budget, where a start-up must accept the possibility that their customers have a variety of purchase options, including things that are different but funded from a common budget. Think of this as comparable to the decision you make as a family on whether to redo the basement or go on vacation. These are competing budget options but would not normally be viewed as competing products.

To illustrate, suppose that a start-up sells office supplies. The administrative budget that services office supply purchases would likely also include various unrelated items such as team training and business travel. Thus, the office supply start-up would need to recognize that it is actually competing for funding with educational platforms and industry conferences—two businesses that have zero to do with office supplies other than a shared budget.

Our advice for start-up companies in this area is simple: Keep an active and ongoing discussion with your customers, and you will get a better feel for how they allocate budget. You will also come to understand the various trade-offs that exist in the decision making around your solution. We also strongly advise start-ups to maintain an active customer advisory board precisely for issues such as this.

Many start-ups use their boards to brag about their accomplishments. This is rational if the board can fire you at will. But I would rather you find a way to utilize your board to do what they do best—that is, offer judgment and perform governance. They will also know how to help you jockey the minefields that emerge in the context of how customers manage their budgets.

CASE STUDY: HYDROSTOR VERSUS AMBRI

Two new companies we have studied in our advisory practice at TAG are Hydrostor and Ambri. Our work with Ambri spanned both cyber-security and climate science, so we were able to gain some insight into their business. Hydrostor also spent time with our analysts explaining its business, and we were impressed with its approach to compressed-air energy storage. Let's review how both companies have been indirect budget competitors.

Ambri was created as a liquid battery technology company that supports long-duration energy storage applications. Ambri batteries were designed to operate at a staggering 500°C to 700°C (hotter than the surface of Mercury). In contrast, Hydrostor offers an energy storage solution that is focused on enabling transition to a more sustainable electricity grid. Its approach is based on using compressed air, which is obviously different than Ambri's solution.

Both companies targeted the energy storage business. But when we asked Ambri about its competitors, it would inevitably describe doing battery-related innovation. When we asked Hydrostor about its competitors, it would discuss compressed-air vendors. These are rational responses to questions about competition—and their perspectives are 100 percent accurate about their direct competitors.

But the competitive analysis must also include the plethora of diverse start-ups and established vendors supporting a variety of energy storage solutions, most of which use methods that are different from those of Ambri or Hydrostor. The leadership teams for these two example companies are capable and open to the idea that this expanded view of competition should be factored into the marketing equation.

It is thus recommended that you also keep an open mind—and remember that the budget allocation for your product might not come only from direct competitors. The budget allocation could be pulled from products that are quite different from yours. Recognition of this fact will serve to improve your messaging.

A not-so-subtle reminder of the challenges of getting into the start-up business is the fact that Ambri filed for bankruptcy in 2024 after a failed $300 million series F round. You need to acknowledge the struggles of many good early-stage companies in order to avoid the common trap of complacency. The start-up business can be harrowing.

INACTION COMPETITION

The most insidious competitor for most start-ups is the invisible one—namely, the unfortunate case in which a buyer chooses to do nothing. This option is always troublesome for start-ups because many buyers view this minimalist scenario as being the cheapest, easiest, and lowest risk option. It is up to start-up teams to help their customers understand that if they do nothing, this will have a negative impact.

In cybersecurity, this approach has been lampooned as so-called fear, uncertainty, and doubt (FUD), and salespeople have been encouraged to avoid this strategy. Our coaching at TAG is for start-ups to be honest in their assessment regarding nonuse of their product, regardless of whether this involves FUD. If buyers really should be fearful of some problem, for example, cyberhacks, then it is reasonable to point this out.

We have looked at start-ups such as SilviaTerra, which is involved in forest management with an emphasis on preventing fires. Obviously—and I mean obviously—these types of start-ups can, should, and must point out the dangers of forest fires to drive sales. It would be ridiculous for them to do otherwise, especially as fires in Canada and the United States continue to pollute the air across both countries.

Is this FUD? Yes. Is this effective? Yes. I recommend that you go ahead and use this approach as long as it is honest and accurate.

COMPETITION ROAD MAP FOR START-UPS

The complexity of options regarding competition can be daunting—and it might not be immediately evident how a founding team should navigate the waters of their competing entities. To help with this process, I have developed a simple road map that can be followed by founding teams and their strategists to review their competitive landscape and determine the path forward that offers the highest probability of success.

Look at the road map in figure 4.2 and try to interpret each of the lanes in the context of your start-up. Think of this as a preliminary exercise to getting the real work done. Once you have developed a reasonable understanding of your own competitive situation, then you can begin to create long-term strategies (one to two years for an early-stage start-up) and near-term tactics (more like weeks, days, and even hours) that will address your competition.

Also keep in mind when reviewing the road map that you can and will have to navigate multiple lanes at once. For example, you will have several or even all these competitive situations arise during your early-stage growth. Both inaction and budget competition will be present, for example, for as long as you are in business, not just during the early growth years. You will have to handle multiple competitive cases at once.

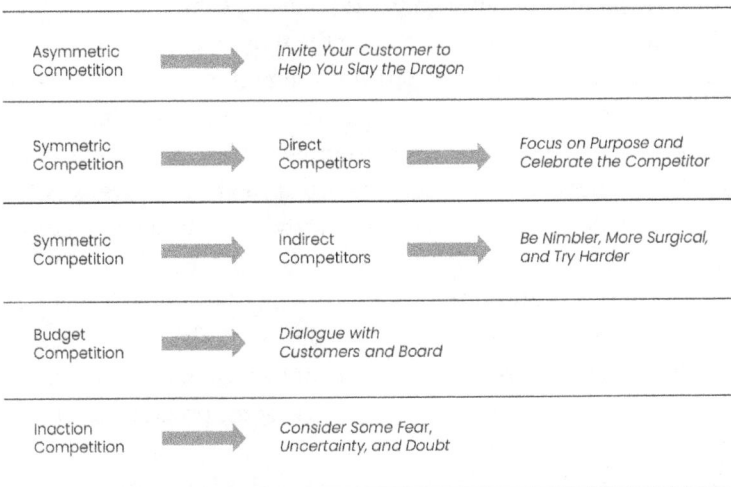

Asymmetric Competition	→	Invite Your Customer to Help You Slay the Dragon		
Symmetric Competition	→	Direct Competitors	→	Focus on Purpose and Celebrate the Competitor
Symmetric Competition	→	Indirect Competitors	→	Be Nimbler, More Surgical, and Try Harder
Budget Competition	→	Dialogue with Customers and Board		
Inaction Competition	→	Consider Some Fear, Uncertainty, and Doubt		

Figure 4.2 Start-up competition road map

One question I often get with this road map is, "Why don't you include indirect competitors who might be asymmetric (that are larger)?" Our observation is that the effects of a larger competitor that is not directly offering a similar product to a start-up will be more muted. A start-up delivering meals to clients might see Uber as a major asymmetric competitor because it might be similar. But they probably wouldn't include Walmart, which sells groceries in its stores.

If your situation is different, then interpret the road map as you see fit, but we are strongly in favor of the founding team and marketing staff completing this exercise. It will either confirm your existing approach to the competition or it might help to identify a better path toward handling that always uncomfortable feeling of having to address someone who is competing for your customers.

PARTNERS ARE USUALLY WOLVES IN SHEEP'S CLOTHING

One final point regarding competition involves the concept of partner, which, in my opinion, is among the most misunderstood business concepts in the entire start-up community. I estimate that at least twice per day for the past eight years, our analysts have heard start-ups tell us that they are partnering with some massive company, prominent vendor, or larger start-up, and we always ask what the partnership actually means. The answers are usually vague and unclear.

In a start-up context, a partnership usually means that both products have been tested to show that they basically work together, which is hardly a partnership. It is an integration. Partnership can also mean that the start-up participates in some program developed by a larger company such as Microsoft to guide how smaller companies can operate in their ecosystem. Again, this is not a partnership. It is membership, along with others, in a program.

In some partnering cases that I hear from founders, some larger company like a major vendor or large integrator has a gap in their portfolio, and they have approached one or more smaller vendors to announce that their solution could potentially fill the void should some customer make that request. For example, in IT systems management, we often see smaller IT product vendors announce a partnership with a larger provider such as ServiceNow or SolarWinds.

What this actually means is that if a customer of these larger companies would like to insert the smaller vendor's solution, that would be something they could do without a lot of additional paperwork. This is a useful scenario for the customer, but we coach start-ups to be careful here. The larger partner is more often than not a wolf in sheep's clothing, so to speak. Your start-up might be serving as a means for market testing some solution.

If things go well on a few initial engagements, then the larger company will develop a similar solution and side-step your so-called partnership. And I know what you are thinking: Perhaps this will be the first step toward an acquisition, thus fulfilling your dream of a lucrative exit. While this might be true, we advise and coach caution because this can be extremely dangerous territory.

5

WHAT IS YOUR KEY ADVANTAGE?

You will need a great product/market fit to be successful in your start-up. This is not up for debate. Marc Andreessen, developer of the world's first successful web browser and one of the most successful entrepreneurs in the world, has made this case repeatedly in blogs and talks. He has said that, regardless of your team, your funding, or your background, there is no success if there is no market. And my experience at TAG is consistent with his observation.

What this means is that your first key advantage must be that you are providing a product or service to buyers that fits well into a healthy market. If this is not the case, then you will likely fail, even if you believe in your heart that you are creating something new that will drive a brand-new buying category. Remember that key advantages, as we will discuss below, are irrelevant if you do not have a good product/market fit.

A start-up usually succeeds because there is a good market, and it happens to be in a good position to address the needs of this market. You should thus interpret our guidance below on key advantages in this context: If you can establish product/market fit, then several areas must be examined to determine your unique suitability to address this great market to which you have devoted your time and energy.

Before we get into these key advantages, I suspect you are waiting for the recipe to determine how to confirm great product/market fit. I am sorry to say that there is no such procedure or equation—and ChatGPT also will not provide an answer that you can cut and paste to answer this question. Determining whether your product addresses a growing market is like catching a wave as a surfer. It is highly dependent on timing, and that can be tough to control.

Perhaps the best advice is that you need to watch existing markets for trends, listen to experts offering opinions, read everything you can find from *Wired* magazine to *The Economist*, talk frequently to customers and buyers, and do everything you can to predict accurately where things will go in a given area. The key issue here is timing. Your widget might be a flop today, but the next big thing in five years.

Even if you do everything right—from belief systems to value propositions, and so on—every early-stage start-up is still a massive roll of the dice. The problem of timing to ensure product/market fit introduces a great deal of uncertainty into your start-up process, but it is the truth. It helps to explain why there are no step-by-step guides (including this book) to business success.

Everything involves doing whatever you can do to improve and even stack the odds. This chapter includes some areas in which start-ups can optimize their chances of success by focusing on their key advantages—but even these important differentiators do not change the basic start-up business fact that without proper timing and a good product/market fit, you still might struggle.

DOMAIN INSIDER KNOWLEDGE

When meeting with a start-up founder working in some highly domain-specific area, it is natural to presume that they have expertise in that area. For example, if I meet a start-up founder working in nuclear fusion, then my presumption is that they studied physics. And there might be a founding team that includes a domain expert, but this is essentially the same thing. The team must include domain expertise.

You increase the odds of having the right domain expertise when you are a team of two or more founders. I have seen this work nicely as long as the founding team is 100 percent on the same page. We at TAG have watched two founders openly disagree about foundational issues. Debate is good, but only on a common base of understanding. If you are a multi-person founding team, then make sure you are unified.

Regardless of the size of the founding team, it is more than just an advantage to include founders with domain-specific knowledge: It is as close to a requirement as I've ever seen in the start-up business. Domain expertise avoids the situation where a neophyte chases some area because it is hot. That is, in my opinion, a recipe for failure in most cases.

We sometimes use the term "market opportunism" to refer to the unwelcome case where there is no domain expertise on the founding team. This sometimes involves the familiar serial entrepreneur, who goes from one start-up to the next, picking up a new sports car after each exit. I've run into such folks many times, and they tend to apply a formula from one area to another. They do a real estate start-up and exit, then they do a tech start-up and exit, then they do a food delivery start-up and exit, and so on.

These types of start-up founders tend to possess general management or financial skills and then hire domain expertise onto the team. Many software start-ups, for example, are created by people who do not code. These types of founding teams focus on creating balance, often with the assistance of a venture capital team with a large contact list. It often results in one cofounder as the executive and perhaps another as the product domain expert.

Investors love serial entrepreneurs because such individuals and groups presumably have the wherewithal to jockey the obstacles in the start-up process to ensure a successful exit. Maybe the process is self-perpetuating because if investors are giving money primarily to serial entrepreneurs, then they will be the ones with the money to at least have a chance of success.

At TAG, however, we always prefer to see domain expertise driving the purpose statement for the founding team. Show us the group of Big Company scientists who decided to take their expertise away from their greedy employer to develop a start-up and we'll be eager to hear their story. We obviously look for *product/market fit*, but once this has been confirmed, then domain expertise will drive points in the success column in our book every time.

A scenario we like to pose to founders is this: Imagine the government passing a law tomorrow that you personally were not allowed to make another penny of salary for the rest of your life. Assume that you have enough money to live, but that you were 100 percent free to spend your time doing whatever you liked for the rest of your life. What would you do each day in this scenario? Would you play golf or tennis, or fish?

Golf and tennis are the types of answers we hear from serial entrepreneurs, but almost never from domain experts. If I were in this situation, then I'd still be on Zoom calls with start-ups, and I would still be teaching and coaching enterprise teams, and I would still be typing these words into this chapter. I created my start-up because it is what I do. I don't have to wait for a start-up exit to play golf.

CASE STUDY: TRUEFORT APPLICATION SECURITY

During his time as an executive working in application security at JPMorgan Chase, my friend and former student Sameer Malhotra developed deep expertise and understanding of the challenges that faced by enterprise teams, especially in banking, in protecting their applications when they ran in data centers or in the cloud. I watched as he and his cofounder Nazario Parsacala, also a banking expert, make the decision to take the plunge with their start-up TrueFort.

I remember visiting the company's early offices in Jersey City, and if you had had Steven Spielberg put together a vision of what a start-up outfit should look like, their offices fit the bill. The rooms were crowded with equipment, and developers were hunched over their desks working hard. The conference room looked more like a storage room. And finding parking in front of their building was nearly impossible.

The place was electric, however, and as the founding team explained to me what they were doing, it was so exciting to absorb their strategy and to feel the energy of domain experts building something that they wish they had had when they were in the role of application security practitioners. In other words, they were building something they would have liked back when they were buyers of similar products.

But, as we have explained throughout this book, start-up companies are harrowing endeavors. And in 2025, TrueFort decided to suspend its operations. Readers should understand that even with deep levels of expertise and capable founders, if the product/market fit is not right, then the business will not succeed. We have every confidence that this amazing founding team will be back in the saddle again soon. We wish them nothing but the best.

ALLIANCES

As alluded to earlier, my experience is that claims of partnerships are overplayed by most start-ups. There are relationships that can be beneficial to founders, however, and we refer to these as alliances. In most contexts, an alliance is a connection that can be leveraged for mutual benefit. This implies that both parties should find value in the relationship, but the connection does not have to be symmetric in terms of the size, scope, and scale of the two connected entities.

For example, an executive might depart from a large company to create a start-up. Assuming the exit was on reasonable terms, an important alliance emerges between the departed executive and the colleagues who remain at the larger company. This involves an alliance between two entities who are not similar in any way, shape, or form. A new start-up does not resemble a company full of executives, practitioners, and other resources.

But an alliance will emerge nevertheless. Whereas the departing founder can utilize the relationship to grow their business, the larger company might also benefit by having access to this new independent voice or set of eyes and ears with a more externally focused perspective. Such an alliance can help both parties with market studies, competitive research, or other types of useful support.

Another key alliance worth mentioning here is the channel alliance, also known as business alliance. Notice that I didn't say channel partner because this is usually not an accurate description of the relationship—as illustrated in figure 5.1. Value-added resellers (VARs), for example, are go-between suppliers of a portfolio of different product and service options, often marked up with add-on support, consulting, or other features.

Channel Partnerships	Business Alliances
Transactional	Relationship-Based
Channel Owns Customer	Start-up Owns Customer
Pass Through Benefit for Start-up	Mutual Benefit for Both
Start-up Easily Replaced	Relationships Not Easily Replaced
Drives Growth If Done Right	*Drives Growth If Done Right*

Figure 5.1 Difference between channel partnerships and channel alliances

Using a VAR can be a powerful approach for vendors, such as small and medium-sized businesses (SMBs) or consumers, trying to cover a wide market. It can also be a huge help when trying to sell to organizations that have baroque procurement procedures, such as federal government agencies. In these cases, identifying and selling through a channel is an excellent idea. We do this frequently at TAG.

But you must be careful because VARs and other channel alliances create a layer of obfuscation between you and the actual buyer or user of your product. In the best case, you will lead or at least participate in the support of customers using your product. In the worst case, you will be nothing more than a wholesale provider of a solution that your channel uses to develop and nurture relationships with their own customers. You become part of a so-called pass-through.

Such a transactional fit can also lead to product or service replacement, especially if the channel plays a large role with the customer. This could be the VAR providing day-to-day support of your product. Again, alliances are important as long as they create value for all parties in a relationship. But if the value tips away from your team toward some other company, then you must find a way to restore the balance.

CASE STUDY: KPMG's AI START-UP

I first met Jonathan Dambrot in the mid-2000s when he was running a start-up called Prevalent that focused on the growing cyber-risk of third-party suppliers to enterprise customers. Prevalent became a customer of TAG, and we enjoyed helping them grow. Their focus on third-party security was a master class in timing a market perfectly. They emerged onto the scene at the same time that all our customers were asking about third-party risk.

Dambrot later moved to KPMG to help them grow their own third-party solution. This was a good idea because KPMG developed a unique offering in this area. But Dambrot was soon sharing with me his ideas on how to get right back into the start-up game (it's tough to get start-ups out of your system). The area in which he was interested in targeting was the cross product between security and AI.

Dambrot shared with our TAG team his early design plans for Cranium, the new start-up, and they were exciting indeed. The team was to focus on providing and overlaying security onto the emerging pipeline used in businesses to leverage AI for analytics and other purposes. But one of the most unique aspects of the company was that it was done as a spin-off from KPMG.

Spinning off had many benefits. First, it helped with financing because KPMG maintained a slice of ownership in the new company. The arrangement also preserved vital alliances that Dambrot and his team had developed within KPMG over the years. This helped attract early adopter customers and also helped Dambrot get feedback from trusted individuals and groups who understood the context of the new company and what it was hoping to accomplish.

As this book goes to press, Cranium continues to grow and benefit from these business alliances with the larger KPMG community.

UNIQUE ACCESS TO CUSTOMERS

An additional advantage we generally seek to find when reviewing start-ups involves how the company will gain access to customers. This seems obvious, but it's amazing how frequently we hear pitches from start-ups that include zero guidance on how they will locate, contact, and initiate a sales discussion with target customers. Without such a plan, it is inconceivable that anything will get off the ground.

We hear the dreaded dog food market story frequently, and it goes roughly as follows. The dog food market in North America is a staggering $36.4 billion per year, and much of it involves inefficient distribution through traditional channels. An online dog food business should be able to capture easily 1 percent of this market, right? One percent is just a tiny slice and that will drive $364 million, which makes for a lovely start-up revenue.

Many start-up companies proceed along these lines, only to find that they actually capture something more along the lines of 0 percent of the market. Why? Because they do not have a good means for reaching customers. A start-up cannot magically obtain a slice of a target market. A start-up needs a plan to develop unique access to customers, perhaps through the connections of the founders or investors.

Unique access to customers often emerges when executives in business or government start a company that sells back to the exact teams they had been interacting with (or managing) previously. Such access represents an unfair advantage over competing firms that do not share these legacy relationships. When a military general retires and starts a company, then selling back into the military represents an unfair but powerful advantage.

Another approach to customer access involves channel alliances, albeit with the pros and cons discussed earlier in this chapter. But when it works, it can establish a connection to customers. Many years ago, for example, a security company called Tanium created an offer that piggybacked McAfee security deployments. This became an excellent distribution channel for Tanium, which grew quickly, partly because they obtained great access to target enterprise customers through McAfee.

CULTURAL CONNECTION TO CUSTOMERS

The next advantage a start-up team might possess involves a shared culture with its target customers. The idea is that businesses and consumers generally prefer to buy products or subscribe to services from people and teams who have a culture that is either consistent with their own or that gives the appearance of being attractive. If you need a definition of culture, think shared norms.

Imagine that a start-up created by former U.S. marines is set up to sell to current U.S. marines. Ponder the significance of the shared culture here in getting a deal. Marines will generally buy products and services from those who share their culture. Buyers and sellers will almost always come together under shared belief systems and common cultural norms.

I had the privilege to meet Biz Stone and Jack Dorsey when they were starting Twitter. Our meeting was in the context of a Bell Labs video series I was producing on innovations in technology. I never expected their service to grow into what it has become, but it was clear to me that these founders were interesting and certainly different, as if Spielberg had summoned them from central casting. I believe their growth was heavily influenced by this culture.

Another example is the CEO of NVIDIA, Jensen Huang. He built the most amazing company, perhaps in history. He always wears a black leather jacket; it is tough to find recent photos of this technologist not wearing his uniform—and that is exactly what it is, a uniform. But it is effective in sending cultural signals to buyers, pundits, and Wall Street.

Regional culture can also make a start-up appealing to a buyer. Tennessee-based data protection company Sertainty, for example, is run by a team of experts who exude Tennessee culture. The start-up is led by my friend Greg Taylor and has worked with TAG for years. I have visited them in Nashville on multiple occasions. They are awesome and welcoming people, and anyone who enjoys that region will have fond thoughts of this fine company.

PERSONAL GIFT OF FOUNDERS AND EXECUTIVES

Having a truly gifted founder, CEO, or otherwise iconic individual in your start-up is an amazing asset. It lends immediate credibility to your start-up and can open many doors. Name recognition is such as challenge for start-ups, and a famous founder can address this effectively. But having a famous leader comes with a strong warning: The famous founder has to be available to customers.

I know of one start-up that has an iconic academic founder from a major engineering school. Everyone knows him, and the sales team brings up this person's name frequently during our advisory sessions. But we never see this famous person, presumably because his interests lie elsewhere, he is busy teaching, or we are just not important enough for his time.

I would say that this is almost worse than not having him as part of the founding team because it makes us feel unimportant. Every time a start-up invokes their founder during a discussion with a customer, the immediate thought that arises in that customer's mind is that the famous person does not value this discussion sufficiently to be present. Contrast this with a reference to the famous founder who is right there supporting the customer interaction. The presence of a famous founder makes a huge difference.

For online services, B2C offerings, or other consumer products and services, having a famous founder is also true—but it manifests in different ways. If the founder is someone that can be admired uniformly, then their product or service will benefit from having them as part of the leadership team. The surrogate for being present with buyers is being present on social media, at events, and on YouTube or TikTok videos. Famous business-to-consumer (B2C) founders must also connect with buyers.

I had the wonderful opportunity to spend time recently with Tim Berners-Lee, the inventor of the World Wide Web. Berners-Lee is now part of a start-up called Inrupt that is designed to help people own and manage their personal data. While customers might not be lucky to get a private audience with perhaps the most iconic technologist of our time, his reputation helps the company immeasurably.

In contrast, take Elon Musk and his controversial life, career, and approach to business and politics. Some are sure to find him a spectacular inspiration. Many of our employees at TAG have been fans of Musk. But not everyone feels this way, especially after the billionaire ceremoniously bought Twitter and began to dismantle the company. He is a truly polarizing individual.

I used to tweet every day, and I haven't done so, not even once, since Musk took over the company. I understand that this might be irrational, but I choose, primarily because of Musk, not to use Twitter. I'm also in the market for an electric vehicle and I'll let you guess which company I am not looking at.

Keep in mind that famous founders are a double-edge sword. If they are present and connect with buyers in a positive manner, the results can be amazing. But if they are not present, or they turn off buyers through polarization, then the results can be unpredictable.

CASE STUDY: NIR ZUK AND PALO ALTO NETWORKS

I first met Nir Zuk many years ago when he was one of the first engineers to develop, use, and deploy internet firewalls using a method he developed called stateful inspection. He was an inspirational cybersecurity technologist then, and throughout his career, he has continued to be positioned with the right company, developing the most useful technology, and doing so with deep expertise.

He is best known as the founder of Palo Alto Networks, an iconic company with revenues of $50 billion. Palo Alto Networks has been a customer of TAG for years, and Zuk has been generous to me personally with his time. He has often taken me through his innovative thinking, and despite my own involvement in the field, I always learn something new from him. This is how an iconic founder should operate, and it helps explain why the company has thrived.

I have been lucky to have had repeat access to this iconic founder. Not all Palo Alto Networks customers do simply because there aren't enough hours in the day. Companies like Palo Alto Networks have to be thoughtful and careful about how they make a prominent individual available to their customers. Otherwise, some customers might feel neglected.

Keynotes at conferences are nice ways to allow customers to hear directly from famous founders. Video and social media also work well, as do podcasts. Regardless of the approach taken, founders who are well known must work hard to make buyers feel that they have been invited into a private community of shared belief with the famous individual when they purchase the start-up's product or service.

ABILITY TO ATTRACT THE BEST TEAM

A final advantage is that founding teams must determine a means for attracting the best talent to their team. And this should never include the use of headhunters. Except for special, isolated instances, usually involving senior executives, a headhunter is a poor way to find good start-up talent. Founding teams have frequently shared horror stories with me of terrible (sometimes unethical) experiences with headhunters. Please stay away.

Rather than rely on search firms or headhunters, founding team should have a network that they can rely on. Venture capital funders are often helpful in this regard, although their suggested (sometimes demanded) personnel changes are not always 100 percent welcomed by start-up founders and managers. Regardless of the specifics, there should be an organic network from which to attract talent into the early-stage company.

At TAG, several members of our sales and leadership team come from AT&T, where I served for so many years. I know these individuals and I trust them based on decades of interaction. My ability to reach back into a firm where I was employed for decades to attract talent has been a great benefit. I also teach wonderful graduate and undergraduate students each semester, and many of our best developers are cherry-picked from the classroom.

The topic of diversity in hiring is a tough area because everyone knows what how incredibly valuable it is to have a diverse leadership team, management team, and practitioner team. Varying the backgrounds, cultures, experiences, and other attributes of your staff is a powerful way to ensure that decisions and work activities benefit from a variety of perspectives. I favor diversity, and we coach its benefits to TAG customers.

Start-ups are often more effective, however, with a team of individuals of common background, culture, experience, and other attributes. I know this is a controversial statement, but in my view, diversity should be one of the most important goals as the company grows, if only because it is such a powerful approach to building a resilient community.

But for small entities, say, fifty people or less, this might be more aspirational than required. We coach our start-ups to hire the best people during the early stages, always with an eye to diversity and inclusion. If you can get capable team members with diverse backgrounds, no staffing approach is better. But tiny companies might struggle to do this effectively, so they should not beat themselves up over the issue.

The bottom line with respect to diversity in a start-up is the following: Focus on hiring the best possible people in the early stages of your growth, and make sure they are aligned 100 percent with your vision, your approach, and your culture. Once you begin to grow, you will have the opportunities to develop that wonderful and inclusive ecosystem of varying perspectives, backgrounds, and approaches to business.

6

HOW ARE YOU FUNDED?

When meeting with the founders of a start-up, I always ask them about funding. And never once has any founding team offered anything but an upbeat response. They point to their angel investor, to their seed funding from a group of investors, or to their completed series A round from a well-known venture capital team. We do occasionally run into the bold bootstrapped start-up that probably uses services to fuel new product development.

Even start-ups with no funding or clear prospects for funding respond with an enthusiastic and positive response. They talk about meetings they are having and the amazing feedback they've gotten in the funding process. And I guess it makes sense: A start-up is an irrational business decision by any measure, so only the most optimistic leaders will be attracted to such a high-risk and high-stakes game. Enthusiasm certainly abounds when we ask about funding.

My follow-up to the question about funding is always the same—and to my delight, the responses from almost 100 percent of founding teams is the same. I ask the founders to explain the purpose of their funding: "Why are you raising funds?" And, as if they all are reading from the same hymnbook, they respond to this question with the same one-word answer: growth.

HOW DOES AN EARLY-STAGE START-UP GROW?

Our baseline is thus predictable: Every start-up has some means for generating funds, and every start-up is obsessed with growth. This is not only fine; it is advised. The purpose of an early-stage start-up should be to grow, and such uniformity of response leads me to believe that founding teams are at least consistent in what they hope to achieve with their funding. Perhaps the most apt question, however, is "How will you grow?"

I then request insight into how the start-up plans to grow. They respond with a smooth growth curve, usually sloping up toward some sort of hockey-stick shape at the end. The start-up then explains that successive rounds of funding will drive this curve. They will start with initial dollars, add people, and then get more dollars, and add more people, and so on. It all looks nice and clean—at least on PowerPoint.

Of course, things never go this way. Start-up growth goes up and down, and this way and that. It shifts and starts; the founders will have periods of euphoria and periods of doom and gloom. Once a start-up manages to reach and then cross the chasm, the founders clean up their growth story: Every growth story is smooth and predictable after the fact, but during the flight, it is 100 percent turbulence.

Here is a visual thought exercise that I hope is helpful: Sit down right now and diagram your expected start-up growth curve on a piece of graph paper, then perhaps violently shake the table underneath your pencil as you write. The resulting messy graph will resemble what to expect in your early years much more accurately than any carefully charted course. (It's a thought exercise: You don't really have to write on a shaking table.)

START-UP FUNDING PURPOSE

We have acknowledged that growth is acceptable as the main purpose for obtaining funding. It is useful to dig deeper into why you are actually obtaining funding. I suspect that the honest answer for most founding teams is fear. By having a safety net of dollars supporting the company, the appearance of lower risk emerges for many founding teams. This hope is unfortunately unfounded. You cannot push away risk by taking money, not in a million years.

Regardless of your funding situation, the only way to reduce your business risk is to obtain customers and delight them. If you want to sleep well at night as a founder, focus less on obtaining funding and focus much more on obtaining an initial set of buyers, then keep them delighted through shared beliefs, wonderful value, and consistent concierge support.

Which brings me to another good answer to what a start-up should be doing with its money. Apart from the stealth start-up needing up-front investment dollars to pay developers to sit in a garage and secretly code the next big thing, I firmly believe that investment funds should be used for two things: The first is to obtain customers, and the second is to delight and keep them. These are the reasons for obtaining funding, and it is how you grow.

This notion of obtaining customers is often expressed as only a secondary concern for many founding teams. Too many start-ups view customers as a distraction that takes their attention away from building an amazing product that will eventually take off—not now, but later. It is easier to take dollars and point to the future. When you do this, you do not have to deliver now. But businesses must have customers.

This warped view of always looking to the future is unfortunately reinforced by certain (not all) elements of the investment community. Venture capital teams often place small value on how happy an initial set of customers might be and larger value on the wondrous growth prospects of some developing platform. They surely have every right to take this future-oriented position. After all, they are putting up the money, and they want to optimize their aggregate return.

Venture capital firms do not expect all the start-ups they fund to succeed. Rather, they are set up for a small percentage to take off like crazy, generating a return that justifies the entire portfolio.

They are looking for rockets, not bicycles; nuclear bombs, not fire-crackers; smorgasbord meals, not light snacks. They expect a few big wins, and this model means establishing a lineup of companies that will sink or swim (mostly sink).

We have learned so much through our day-to-day associations with ForgePoint Capital, Ballistic Ventures, Evolution Equity, Millennium Technology Value Partners, and many other amazing venture capital and private equity firms. These fine teams have guided us through their process, included us in their company dinners, invited us to speak at their events, and allowed us to ask more questions than would be reasonable in any context.

And we have had the great privilege to work with the portfolio companies of these venture capital teams. We coach them on growth, blog about their platforms, and help them navigate term sheets. Without the assistance of these venture capital firms, private equity teams, and their portfolio start-ups, I would know little about the funding process toward acquisition or initial public offering (IPO) because TAG has not engaged any external funding.

My earlier decades of experience were mostly on the buying side of the equation versus the building and selling. So just like you, I've had to learn the ropes. The venture capital teams have been kind to help.

REVENUE NEUTRALITY

A high percentage of start-up founders claim something called revenue neutrality. This is a euphemism for the claim that they are profitable, whatever that means. It's an interesting notion because everyone knows that venture-funded start-ups are created for sky-rocket growth, not mundane revenue neutrality. Leave that humdrum stuff for the private equity firms, the venture investors claim. And, again, this is a reasonable position for them.

But we see founder after founder make this claim of being either at, or on a path toward, revenue neutrality. This comes up so much

Total Three Year Profit:
Profit 1 + Profit 2 + Profit 3

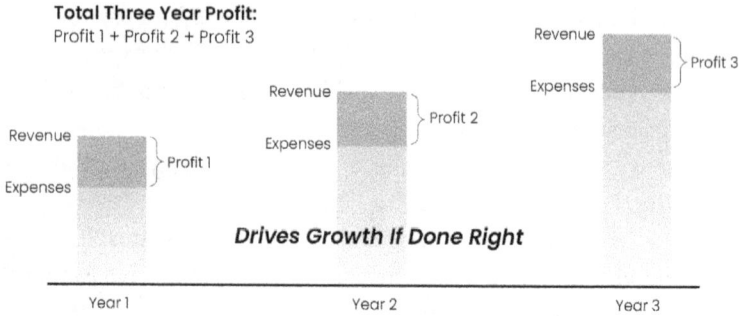

Drives Growth If Done Right

| Year 1 | Year 2 | Year 3 |

Figure 6.1 Bootstrapped start-up income statement model

that it begs some analysis and a couple of diagrams to illustrate. First, let's take the case of a bootstrapped start-up that has taken no investment dollars and that gets to work on day one finding customers and keeping them happy. A simple depiction of their financials might look like the example in figure 6.1.

The figure shows that the so-called income statement model for the bootstrapped firm is revenue positive or profitable by most definitions. That is, the company takes in more than it dishes out over three years. This is how every small business that is not an early-stage, high-growth-oriented start-up works. It's how the diner on the corner and the barber who cuts your hair operate. They take in a certain amount and pay out less. It's simple to say, but tough to do.

But the funded start-up is different. They are given a sometimes considerable amount of money to be used to lubricate the organization for growth. In the worst case, they use this money to create a distorted view of the actual market, for example, using investment to sell hot dogs on the corner for ten cents, so to speak, which will result in growth but not in a market sustainable manner. Figure 6.2 shows the funded income statement model.

If the marketing team removes from the diagram all that messiness about funding and early losses and focuses only on the three-year revenue growth curve, perhaps along with the recognition

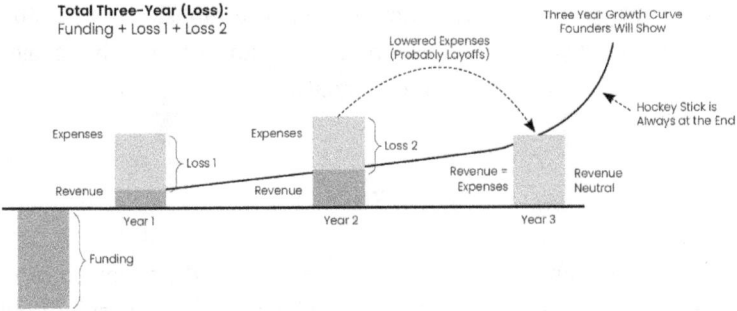

Figure 6.2 Funded start-up income statement model

that the company is now revenue neutral, then they get what I would describe as a jaded view of the company's success (see figure 6.3). Marketing teams often use this diagram in their materials shared with customers. That is why people like me must dig much deeper than the marketing charts to understand the real performance of a start-up in its early years.

Now that we've gotten some high-level cash flow and funding preliminaries out of the way, let's really dig into the various stages of funding that characterize start-ups. As we progress through the chapter discussion, see if you can identify where in the funding life

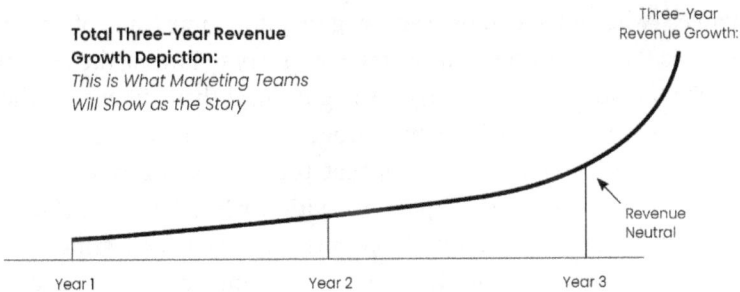

Figure 6.3 Misleading funded start-up revenue growth depiction

cycle your own company might be. Try to establish the pros and cons of where you are and use the descriptions of the other stages to help sharpen your own funding goals.

STEALTH MODE

It is not uncommon for our team to be contacted by venture capital groups or by some highly connected expert in a particular field to let us in on some stealth mode company working on the next big thing. When we agree to chat with these stealth mode founders (after executing a formal nondisclosure agreement [NDA], of course), we tend to be given only a surface overview of what the founding team is working on.

We understand that some innovations do require time to nurture and develop and that there is often great benefit in working on a development program in stealth. The mystique regarding working-in-stealth mode is perhaps worth the trouble of trying to keep the toothpaste in the tube, so to speak. (We do run into some very funny situations where baroque agreements are used for us to pinky-swear to tell no one of the stealth innovation in progress.)

Our observation, however, is that too many stealth mode companies are set up in this manner because the founding team has no time or inclination to speak with customers. You should guess (correctly) that I do not consider this a great idea. Our coaching to stealth companies (when we spend time advising their founding team, often for free) is that the sooner you can tell your story to buyers, the better.

Even if you are creating something magical that will change the world, such as producing power from fusion or stopping hackers using robots, our experience is that these ideas are often more dream than reality. Developing a solution while interacting with customers seems a better notion to me. Just like overclassification tends to be a problem in the intelligence community, being overly stealthy is a similar problem in the start-up community.

My advice is that if you must be work in stealth, then don't make it a habit. Get out quickly and start working with customers. That is the advice we give every day to teams in this mode.

EARLY STAGE

It's most exciting to run into start-ups in the early stage, and by this, we mean companies that are either bootstrap funded using founder money, angel funded, or using some small initial seed investment from family and friends or from a venture capital firm. Our focus in this book and the focus of our practice at TAG, of course, is mostly on early-stage companies, so this is our own bread and butter, so to speak.

The founders of early-stage start-ups are usually eager to get their new company off the ground. Their enthusiasm and excitement are catching. When I'm in a bad mood, nothing cheers me up more than listening to a start-up founder explain their vision of growth. And they come in every size and shape—with enthusiasm as the common denominator.

The canonical presumption has always been that seed-stage founders are young, just out of college, and working in a garage or basement. This is the Facebook version of the start-up—kids coding furiously while chugging caffeinated drinks and eating junk food. Our observation is that this is almost never the case. Most early-stage companies that we run into tend to understand how to conduct their business in a reasonably serious and orderly manner.

Most have a PowerPoint presentation that lays out a serious problem or a gap in some market and how their platform, system, or other solution addresses this problem or fills the gap. I often get the sense that the founders have watched the same YouTube videos on how to develop a pitch presentation because most of their slides look so eerily similar. Many even use the same AI-based Microsoft Designer formatting.

Our guidance might not be entirely consistent with the advice that the earliest start-ups get from their actual venture capital firms. Our advice here is independent of any bias to the reader. That is, we are offering guidance here that we hope you will take as completely unbiased.

Recall that the goal of the venture capital firm is to optimize its aggregate return, not to make sure that there are "no start-ups left behind," so to speak. I often wonder if this is not the biggest misconception that start-up founders have about venture capital investors, namely, that investment groups are in place to guide and nurture new companies. They are not; they are in business to make money.

Let's now metaphorically transpose the venture capital ecosystem for early-stage start-ups into a classroom. Imagine in our analogy that a teacher is addressing a new crop of students, perhaps twenty-five in the room. The teacher announces that one or two of them will graduate with honors and be amazingly successful, a few more will graduate and find a place to work, and the rest—most of the students in the room—will drop out.

To make matters worse, the teacher explains that once it is evident which students show the most promise, they will get most of the time and attention, and the others will be pushed out. This is an accurate metaphor, and you should make sure you are okay with this approach if your goal is to obtain external funding. You will be one of the students in this terrifying classroom.

Now suppose that I walk into the classroom and ask you this: "Where are you headed?" I guess the most statistically correct answer would be to say, "I will most likely be dumped from this class." That is the only rational answer if you do the math. Assuming that you are fine with this situation, we believe that the best way to be one of the few elite students who survives this game is to adopt a customer-centric view from the start.

Let me emphasize this point: The best way to survive the challenges of accepting, using, and leveraging venture capital funding to grow is to adopt a customer-centric view of your business from the beginning.

This mindset is not always easy to adopt, especially if the founding team is developing something revolutionary like cell-cultured meats; carbon-free manufacturing; or another highly complex system that demands focused attention on designing, building, and developing the product, system, service, or other innovation. It is all too easy, in these cases, to develop a technology-, platform-, or product-centric view of your start-up.

The nuclear community, for example, includes companies working on safer approaches to conventional fission and companies working on the future use of fusion, which is high risk but has amazing advantages, including no nuclear waste. I've chatted with start-ups in both areas, and the focus is always on the technology, physics, and operation. They rarely think about where they will sell; they think about how to make energy.

Despite the challenges of both types of start-ups, not having a customer-centric view is a mistake. Every start-up must be obsessed with the buying habits of their target customers. This also helps to identify near-term opportunities that can generate cash quickly, without the need for larger investments from venture capital firms. And this can serve as a hedge in case you find yourself unable to grow at a sufficiently fast rate to keep your funding source happy.

If you can support operations through revenue, then you will have greater control of your company. This is anathema for many funding sources who want their start-ups focused on developing products that will scale and not to waste time looking for near-term revenue, especially if this involves services. They call such excursions unnecessary distractions.

But I always coach start-ups to view revenue opportunities as ways to gain control of their future. Businesses exist to make money from customers, not to live off funding from investors. Leave that to the academic groups. This approach might be inconsistent with the aggregate financial objectives of a venture capital firm, but it is nevertheless 100 percent correct with respect to every business that ever existed.

CASE STUDY: REALITY DEFENDER
AND BLACKBIRD AI

Ben Colman is an innovator running a start-up in New York City called Reality Defender. His team develops technology that can help to differentiate deepfake images and videos from real ones—and the definition of fake versus real is harder to express than you would imagine. I have spent several sessions with Colman in our Manhattan office, and he's also come to New York University to brief our students on his work.

The Reality Defender team has shown our team at TAG just how easy it is for someone to take an image of me, for example, and inject it into some other image or video in an unbelievably convincing manner. It's almost chilling how realistic the final images and videos are. I think this general area of deepfake detection is a new frontier and that Reality Defender and its many new competitors such as GetReal Labs (very cool company) will be successful.

We also love new companies like Blackbird AI who are working to detect and deal with contrived narrative attacks, which involve fake information being levied against target executives and companies. The goal is to ruin reputations for business purposes or to demand ransoms. It's a horrible threat, but addressing the problem is a great start-up opportunity.

I bring up these types of companies in the context of early-stage start-up strategy because, when we look at their platforms, we understand immediately their value as growth rockets with the potential for massive adoption. By exposing these types of protections to customers via an application programming interface (API) or general user interface, they can launch to hypergrowth, and this makes them attractive to investors, especially venture capital.

But we also see parallels, where these companies could focus on services, say, for Fortune 500 companies who would like an expert partner on call, so to speak. Thus, if some deepfakes were to emerge, then Reality Defender, GetReal Labs, or Blackbird AI could swoop in quickly with evidence that the images or narratives were fake (assuming that they really were fake). They could charge big dollars for such a service, and it could fund development of the general platform for many years.

And this illustrates a dilemma that many founders have—namely, whether to go the services route, which provides immediate near-term revenue from customers, or to go the product and platform route, which generally requires external funding to support operations while customer adoption is nurtured. The truth is that just about every start-up founder that I speak with thinks of services as a four-letter word.

From a valuation perspective, my colleague Don Dixon from ForgePoint Capital has explained to me that software platform businesses can grab up to seven times their annual recurring revenue in an acquisition, whereas services companies might get less than half that. This explains the four-letter word reaction.

CASE STUDY: NoPALM

I spent a wonderful afternoon recently in Manhattan over sushi bowls with Jeroen Hugenholtz, cofounder of an early-stage start-up from the Netherlands called NoPalm Ingredients. We've worked with his company on strategy and content, and Hugenholtz was in town for meetings—so I took the opportunity to spend time with this superintelligent guy and to discuss how his team might drive toward an initial round of major funding.

His company is focused on sustainable alternatives to palm oil, which might sound mundane at first glance. But when you learn how palm oils are used in food, health, beauty, and cleaning products, you appreciate the impact such oils can have on the environment. Palm oil production harms our air, soil, and water, and it drives tropical deforestation—a problem some estimate as causing as much as 10 percent of the total global warming emissions.

As you might imagine, it is not hard for the employees of NoPalm to explain their "why" statement. They want to save the global environment, which is why climate science start-ups are so exciting. The question is, "How can they translate this intense purpose and belief system into solutions that offer a great value proposition to early innovator and disruptor clients?"

Because NoPalm is a science-oriented type of environment with real experts working together to change the world, it's hard not to fall in love with such a place. But from a business perspective, the question is, "How can NoPalm develop a growth engine that is profitable and that has the scale to take on the large palm oil industry?" This is anything but easy—and NoPalm continues to focus on solving this puzzle.

NoPalm is the classic disrupter taking on bigger companies, using the David and Goliath mission approach. This demands marketing to highlight the good-versus-evil situation. NoPalm will likely begin by establishing a new side-market, so to speak. The messaging is that, if you want a future for our planet, then you should look for products that use NoPalm.

It will be interesting in the coming years to see how this fine company fares. I hope they find a way to at least coexist with the palm oil companies in much the same way vegan restaurants coexist with McDonalds.

SERIES A STAGE

This is perhaps the most interesting of all funding stages in the context of this book because we view this round as driving early-stage companies who have momentum. They now need money to drive scale, to drive scale, however that must be done—and we have devoted much of this book so far to answering that question. We can offer some additional nuanced observations about start-ups as they reach this vital round of financing.

First, we must reinforce the importance of developing a means for the series A start-up to scale to a mass market. Where seed and pre-series A start-ups could get by on innovators and disrupters, the purpose of most series A rounds is to give the start-up sufficient capital to use their momentum to begin planning for scale. One of the factors in such evolution is the shift away from something known as a proof of concept (POC), also sometimes called proof of value (POV).

It is common to encounter an early-stage start-up (and we focus here on business-to-business [B2B] start-ups) with an impressive customer logo chart, the one used to demonstrate how well the start-up has managed to attract initial buyers. When asked about the logo chart, we usually hear two things: First, they will ask that we not repeat the company names on the chart. This usually means that they did not get approval to list the company on the chart (a topic for another book).

Second, and perhaps more important, we find that the logo chart for start-ups is mostly a series of POCs or POVs where the customer is running a trial—perhaps paid and perhaps not—to determine whether the product will work. This is definitely a good situation because every start-up wants as many customers as possible to test their solution. But POCs and POVs can create a misleading revenue profile.

For example, let's start by acknowledging that every pre-series A start-up founder or marketing executive will swear on a stack of bibles that 100 percent of their POCs goes to the next stage. This is nonsense, of course. My perhaps generous view is that, for the typical start-up, maybe half of POCs will move on to a more extensive engagement. This implies that a start-up with ten paid POCs at $100,000 will celebrate $1 million in revenue, but half of these customers will likely go away.

This implies that advancing from innovator and early adopter customers, many of whom will be in paid trials, to the mass market might be the hardest thing a start-up will ever do. It is the reason we still read Geoffrey Moore's *Crossing the Chasm* over three decades after it was written. And it is why I've based my own guidance here on the anticipation of this extremely difficult journey across the chasm. (I'm doing it now at TAG as this book goes to press.)

There are dozens of reasons why early-stage processes do not scale. Let's look at some obvious ones. Supporting a mass market, for example, requires automation. Any manual process used to help users, coddle problem situations, or deploy to a customer site will slow you down and hold you back. This is ironic because it was exactly this concierge treatment that got you to series A and the chasm in the first place.

In telecommunications, for example, scaled support no longer involves speaking with a human being. Instead, you speak with an AI, which is good because we all know that conversational chatbots can be superior to long wait times for a human. But notice the scaling here. Ten customers or 1 million customers can call at the same time and it's really just a job of matching the automation to the expected demand. It's not always perfect for sure, but it's better than trying to handle the volume manually.

Another scaled example is banking. When I started my own career, you were paid on Friday and you would then go to the bank and literally stand on a line to cash your check so that you would have money for the weekend. The lines were long, and it was a major waste of time. And then came automated teller machines (ATMs).

Some aspects of a business cannot be automated. When a key client is having trouble, any good supplier or vendor will reach out and offer human assistance. The sales process should also be face-to-face for large B2B offers. Sales teams and start-up executives need to connect with big business buyers to help them fall in love with the company and share in their belief system. Robots cannot do that, at least not yet.

Notice that most business-to-consumer (B2C) services do not have this issue. They can and do scale and automate their sale process. Of course, they cannot go out and generate more revenue by meeting with prospects. (How would Instagram make sales calls to customers?) Instead, they must advertise, promote, and do everything but stand on their heads to get customers to use the service. It scales, but it's a tough process.

One B2C automation exception involves the sales channel, where the offer is marketed and sold to a channel partner or close alliance. The resulting business chain is often called B2B2C (business to business to consumer), and the originating start-up will most likely be making human sales calls to the human beings at the eventual business distributing to customers. With B2C, scaling is easier said than done. Some processes will remain manual.

One more reminder about automation and scale as a company begins a series A–funded round toward scaled growth: We advise early-stage start-ups to still stand on their heads to make customers happy. But now that you have achieved line of sight with the chasm, you have to begin rethinking this approach. Concierge treatment for all customers does not scale.

The funding alignment during the early stages of growth is roughly consistent with the early stages of funding rounds (figure 6.4). As one would expect, seed, angel, and bootstrap funding come in the earliest stages—and representative amounts might be in the $1 to $3 million range. As a start-up develops traction and approaches the chasm, series A dollars might be as much as $10 to $30 million.

But beware because the external funding process is anything but this simple. Obtaining venture capital funding for a start-up company is an arduous process, one that results in nonfunding decisions for a majority of those who embark on the path. The figures in this chapter run the risk of making the whole thing look easy—but it is not. Even the review sessions can be brutal, leaving founders clinging to anything in sight to keep from wavering.

At TAG, we are lucky that we are not in series A, but we are looking carefully at how our analysts, who give personal service, can scale using automation. This is our challenge as we try to cross the chasm, and it is an exhilarating process. I am glad that it is hard

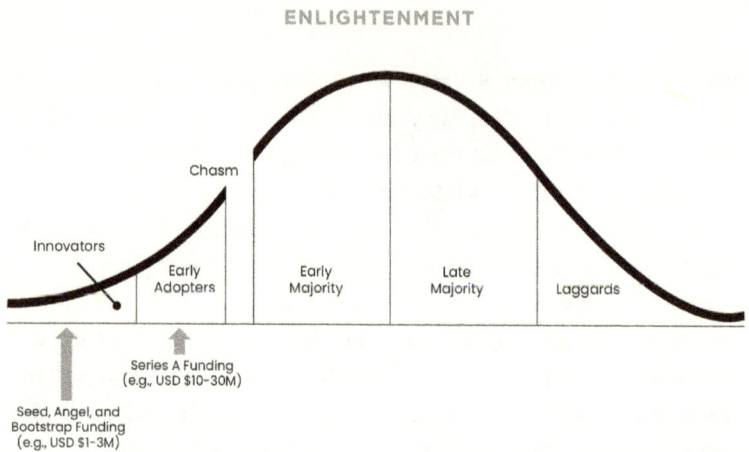

Figure 6.4 Aligning early funding rounds with stages of start-up growth

because it implies that other companies will not make it across the chasm. It's true that not all start-ups make it from limited manual support to scaled, automated growth.

Funding amounts at series A also vary based on industry, region, and sector, so it is probably not helpful to provide a strict range that constitutes funds raised in this phase of the life cycle. But when we advise start-ups who feel flush with cash at this point, we are always careful to remind them that just because they can spend money doesn't mean that they should spend the money.

I know that this might fly in the face of the spend-spend-spend guidance coming from antsy investors demanding rapid growth, but if you have only bad spending options, then we believe it is better to delay than to waste. I have seen too many companies rush out and spend their cash on expensive conference booths, lavish dinners for random attendees, and other clear wastes of money. This is so obviously a bad idea, and yet it is common.

Let's look at the process of recruiting and hiring salespeople with your new series A funding. When you are in a rush to hire, and this is common after a big funding round, what inevitably happens is the so-called alphabet problem, which, if not addressed properly, can lead to nothing but trouble.

If, for example, you have a sales manager who evaluates (in our metaphor) as maybe a B-plus in capability, then that manager should be seeking A-minus and A people. But when you are flush with funding and you rush to hire, then the B-plus person ends up hiring B and B-minus people. And as you go lower in the effectiveness ranking, such people are even more prone to hiring lower-alphabet people—and before you know it, you are a company of C and D employees.

We always advise being very careful with the series A checkbook, especially when hiring or partnering. Never accept lower quality because you are in a rush. It will kill your business from the inside-out. Treat series A dollars as the means by which you can begin scaling, and spend the money wisely. Always stay focused on whether what you are buying contributes directly to achieving your goal of crossing the chasm.

CASE STUDY: AADYA SECURITY

We were pleased to see cybersecurity veteran Raffaele Mautone close his $5 million series A round in 2023 for his start-up company AaDya Security. We advise Mautone and his team on strategy and help to develop technical marketing content for their prospects, and we have been impressed with their fine offer, which bucks the trend of the usual cybersecurity offering presented to us every day.

The AaDya team is trying to help small and medium-sized businesses (SMBs) with cybersecurity, which we believe to be truly important work. Bad cyber actors are happy to go after smaller companies. Even though their budgets might be smaller, SMBs must protect themselves, and that is where AaDya comes in. They are working with buyers who need a solution but who might not fully comprehend this fact.

The start-up problem for AaDya, as any entrepreneur will attest, is that, while it is generally straightforward to find larger customer buyers such as the big banks, it is much more difficult to identify with and connect to smaller businesses. They do not have prominent middle managers who appear at conferences, and they cannot be reached through mass advertisements the way consumers can with TV or internet ads.

One strategy that we have discussed with AaDya stems from the fact that SMBs are open to training and education opportunities. We have coached AaDya to emphasize this aspect of their interaction with SMBs. There is also the potential here for channel alliances. For many series A companies who have not yet established a direct sales force (and who might never do so), the advantage of reaching customers via trusted alliances and channels cannot be overestimated.

SERIES B AND BEYOND STAGE

Once a company has series A funding, several things start to happen. Within the firm, the primary emphasis shifts toward serving mass markets and learning to work with customers on a recurring basis at scale. Series B, C, and D investments can be significant in industries such as cybersecurity, so when big money is involved, start-up founders can become highly vexed, which is where TAG sometimes comes in as an adviser.

We occasionally maintain a consistent advisory relationship with a start-up as it moves from early stage to series A, and then to series B and beyond. But we often find ourselves meeting management teams for the first time who need advisory guidance at these latter stages—and if I had to use one word to describe their honest emotion, it would be "anticipatory."

Once a company has hit this stage and has potentially accepted tens or hundreds of millions in funding, the founders know in their bones that something must soon happen or at least change. Companies do not target these stages to remain there. Rather, they target these stages to plan for an IPO or to become acquired. This implies several things that we advise companies about at this stage.

First and foremost, we coach that they must not take their eye off the ball with their customers. At TAG, we provide research to hundreds of major buyers. We regularly tell enterprise teams, project managers, or other buying stakeholders that when a start-up hits series B and beyond, it is not uncommon for the more mature start-up management team to become severely distracted.

The collective skills to get a company through seed and into a series A growth stage are markedly different than the collective skills to continue growth of a larger start-up with potentially hundreds of employees. Changing the CEO is common if the funding groups dictate, and structural changes are also enacted to prepare the company for continued growth and scale. This can be a tough transition indeed for the original founders.

A popular article from the Harvard Business School that we ask our start-up founders to read is called "The Founder's Dilemma" by Noam Wasserman. In our mind, the paper does the best job anyone has ever done to explain the choices that come from determining whether a founder is motivated only to run things (i.e., to be the king) or to make decisions in the best interests of the company (i.e., to be rich).

This is a difficult decision, one that we ask founding teams to ponder with as much honesty and reflective thought as they can muster. It's a decision that is not unlike one made regarding whether you keep your children under your nose or allow them to set out on their own. These are the types of issues that emerge in these latter stages of a start-up's development—and we view these mature start-ups as the most difficult to coach. It's a tough period, indeed.

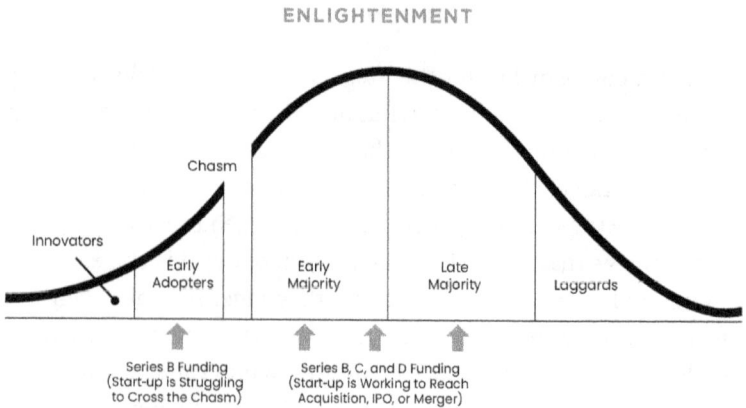

Figure 6.5 Two possibilities for latter-stage funding rounds

The rounds of funding that come after series A—namely, series C, D, and so on (as shown in figure 6.5)—can be roughly categorized into two camps. In the first camp, things are going so well that a post–series A round is completed to throw more lighter fluid on a blazing fire, so to speak. These rounds are celebratory, and they involve using the money, one hopes, to continue pounding the competition into the ground.

But the second type of post–series A round is generally referred to as a "down round" (the term "growth round" is used to make this more positive). Such a funding round is generally viewed as a means for providing emergency maintenance for the original rounds of investment. When we see layoffs done after series B, C, or D rounds, we know that the money is there so that the founders can find the nearest exit.

We have also noticed that latter-stage rounds can be used to give a founding team some more ammunition to take any shot at crossing the chasm. Many start-ups receive their series A, only to find that scaling their start-up was harder than they thought. When this occurs, investors have a choice: They can allow the company to die on the vine, or they can provide some emergency funding to protect their investment.

CASE STUDY: SAFEBREACH

When I first met Guy Berjerano, CEO of start-up SafeBreach, I had a head cold, and all I did during our first meeting in Manhattan was cough and sneeze. I was sure he would not work with me after such a meeting, but I was pleased when his team reached out afterward to talk more. We have since spent several years supporting this fine start-up in its quest to help companies continuously validate that their controls are working properly.

I first became aware of this company three years after it had been founded in 2014 with assistance and support from Shlomo Kramer, a global legend in the field of cyber-investing. Since then, the company has gone through several rounds of funding and growth, up to a recent series D, totaling more than $106 million in investment in the firm. It has been quite successful in raising money.

The question is this: "Having reached series D status and having essentially achieved the goal of helping to create a new category in cyber, what should a vendor such as SafeBreach do next?" The obvious answer is to expand, and in our discussions, we have come to understand that the company's goal is to extend its capability into adjacent areas. Such expansion is common in start-ups after a series D round.

We have assisted the team mostly with the development of technical content in support of this expansion, but I admire the persistence of the leadership team to continue to innovate. We will watch carefully to see how SafeBreach progresses into the coming years because, with their size, scale, and scope, one can only expect an exit.

REVENUE-SUPPORTED START-UPS

The purest and perhaps most challenging form of start-up exists solely on customer revenue. This approach seems almost impossible given the familiar chicken-and-egg argument. How in the world, one might wonder, can a start-up get going with no funding? The answer lies in something called advance planning, which is a fancy way of saying that what appears to be day one for a revenue-supported start-up is anything but day one.

Great founders of bootstrapped companies begin the planning process long before they take the plunge. You have probably heard of the advertising account executives who pull valued clients aside to see if they would be willing to come along for their Jerry Maguire start-up. When sufficient confidence exists that enough clients are available to fund the endeavor, then notice is given, and the day one bell rings.

This underscores the key role that services play in getting a bootstrapped company off the ground. Everyone knows that consultants generate revenue by charging fees to clients; while this model doesn't easily scale to major heights, it is great for getting things started. One or two key clients can provide a bootstrapped company with enough to open a bank account, hire some help, and rent a small office.

Of course, there is also the bank loan route, but I am loathe to recommend it. On a personal note, my wife and I owned a retail store in a mall for years, and we survived on our bank loan, only to sell our lease to the landlord at a nice profit after a decade of operation. Banks can thus play a beneficial role in the start-up process, but founders must understand that whatever comes over as a loan must eventually be paid out, with no exceptions.

Service start-ups that employ auditors, accountants, advisers, trainers, strategists, project managers, and other types of consultants can usually bootstrap without external investment. This situation is a lucky one because most venture capital teams hate these types of companies, which do not include a clear path to scaled growth. Service companies grow linearly, if at all, and fetch much lower acquisition valuations than their product-oriented counterparts.

How do I coach companies who choose to bootstrap? It usually involves two objectives. First, the company should create an organized process for adding staff as new project bids are won. Engineering groups, accounting firms, legal teams, and other professional service companies have done this for years, and it is tried and true. You write proposals with great people waiting in the wings, and when you win the work, you bring them on.

This process is not as exciting as stealth teams coding all night on caffeine to unveil eventually a system that will grab the world by storm. But such growth is a one-in-a-million scenario. The professional services case is far more stable. In fact, you will have great odds, if you work hard, of being in business five years after you start. The services route for a start-up is the nearest thing one will find to a reasonably low-risk option.

The second bit of advice we offer to bootstrappers who are considering jumping into the funding process might be heresy to venture capital teams. Our advice for such companies is that, even if you expect to be some high-flying start-up (not easy from a bootstrapped start), you can and should find a way to include a manageable component of your business that provides a services-based revenue option for your team. I know that your financials are under scrutiny, and I know that you are being told to spend like there is no tomorrow—that is, until they tell you not to spend like there is no tomorrow. Your venture capital team will not like you dabbling in services.

But if the funding spigot stops, like it did in 2023 for most cyber-based companies, when interest rate hikes and an uncertain economy reduced the amount of venture capital available to start-ups, the result in many sectors, including cybersecurity, was layoffs. We watched many great companies panic to the point of sometimes imploding. And this was a shame because the problem was cash flow and not belief systems, value propositions, and the like.

If you have a team of AI experts and your funding is running low, and you are mulling over the need to maybe lay off half your staff, is it really crazy to consider pointing them at a project, say, with a large bank, where they are offering AI-related professional services for a few months. Is this really so bad? I know the venture capitalists will suggest that this takes one's attention away from the main goal, but are layoffs better?

Another possibility is the leave-behind model, which was per-fected at cybersecurity firm Mandiant. The company would offer professional services to companies that had gotten hacked, and after the mess was cleaned up, Mandiant would leave a product behind as an ongoing monitor. This made the relationship sticky, provided annual recurring revenue (ARR), and demonstrated that start-ups can find ways to combine products and services.

As many readers will recall, Kevin Mandia sold his company to Google for $5.4 billion, so I suspect he may have been on to some-thing. The bottom line, I believe, is this: Stiff business formulas for success do not work. Instead, companies must figure out how to delight customers and to do so in a manner that gives them the possibility to grow at scale. This is the closest thing you will find to a workable plan for start-up success.

CASE STUDY: TAG

On the day I started TAG, I sold a contract to a start-up called Catbird for $10,000. I had the contract printed, ready, and signed, and I brought it to their CEO, David Keasey, in a manilla folder the day after my retirement from AT&T. David saw that I had put the contract together carefully, and I explained that this was my first contract ever, and that I'd tell this story and mention his name a thousand times if he'd sign. He did, and I do. (I just did now.)

After getting the signed contract, Keasey sent me a paper check by the U.S. post office. I had been in talks with M&T Bank about joining their board of directors (which I did), so I marched down to the M&T Bank branch in Chester, New Jersey, and I opened a TAG checking account in the amount of $10,000. That first bank receipt was the most beautiful business document that I had ever seen in the world—and over a three-decade career by that time, I had seen some doozies.

Since then, I have not had to put one nickel of my own money into TAG—and today we have a seven-figure balance in our banks (diversified after Silicon Valley Bank, of course), we have roughly forty employees, about a third working part-time, the others working full-time. And we'll do about $5 million in profitable revenue this year if all goes as planned. We are now staring at the chasm, and we are making plans to cross. It requires that we rethink our entire business around scale.

Now, I understand that this is not the type of growth process that makes business headlines like, say, OpenAI. But it is a solid, revenue-supported model where I have curated the business from a scrappy one-person shop to a company with a team that understands the current mission. And we did this without the need for external funding. You can bootstrap to growth but, as I suggested above, you will need to plan ahead, and you will need a good services model.

PLANNING YOUR EXIT OPTIONS: ACQUISITION

The ultimate goal of the growth-oriented start-up is an exit, which can be accomplished through a corporate merger of peers, a corporate acquisition by a larger entity such as a private equity firm, or an IPO. The merger case might not actually constitute an exit per se because the merger of two start-ups creates a newer and stronger entity but one that is still likely focused on acquisition or IPO.

For example, my friend Tamer Hassan, the founder of start-up company Human, merged his start-up company with a competing business, PerimeterX, which resulted in a much more powerful entity. But it has still not made its signature exit. (The topic of exits is beyond the scope of this book.)

My personal experience with start-up acquisition is more on the buying side, having worked through many of them while I was an executive at AT&T. My observation is that the culture of the buying entity and the start-up is the best predictor of whether the acquisition will work. If the cultures are compatible, then things usually work out quite nicely. But when the opposite is true, the results can be terrible.

The acquisition of Cingular Wireless by AT&T was a combination of two technology and service-oriented cultures that shared many common roots, especially a deep focus on and love for networking. By any measure, this was a spectacularly successful corporate acquisition. It worked on so many levels, and most people think of AT&T today primarily as a mobile networking company.

But the famously failed combination of AOL and Time Warner in 2001 is one that business school students still study. Having watched from a ringside seat during that era, my observation is that the internet culture at AOL did not translate to the media culture at Time Warner. This example represents a much larger transaction than a typical start-up acquisition, but the culture issue remains.

CASE STUDY: OBSERVEIT

Mike McKee, former CEO of start-up ObserveIT, was a customer at TAG for many years. We were advisers to his executive and marketing teams, and we spent hours learning, debating, and developing content on their unique approach to behavioral analytics. I remember when McKee told me he was considering accepting an acquisition offer, and he was careful to ensure that he was not compromising the specifics of the deal, including the name of the acquirer.

We agreed to talk in general, and our combined view was that nothing would be more important to driving a successful acquisition than a common culture. For example, would both entities value the same types of contributions? Would both companies value the same types of success cases? Would staff interchange contribute to career growth or would this process be seen as a distraction?

These are the types of soft issues that must be addressed if the goal is a successful merger. I was pleased that, weeks after McKee and I began chatting, the iconic firm Proofpoint was acquiring ObserveIT, resulting in a new offering now called Proofpoint Insider Threat Management. McKee would leave the company after a year or so to get into consulting himself. He is a former pro hockey player, and I'll bet he uses sports analogies in his consulting practice.

PLANNING YOUR EXIT OPTIONS: IPO

If you are considering an IPO as you are reading these words or if this is your major goal as a current start-up founder or executive, then my only guidance is to make sure that you have amazing legal assistance. The IPO process is such a maze of legal, regulatory, financial, human resources, and other complex matters that the skills you used to get your company to this point will be useless during the IPO. The most important aspect of the process is legal.

The good news is that, in almost 100 percent of cases, an IPO only comes after a start-up is really no longer a start-up. At this point, it is a large vibrant firm with a broad and extensive team of seasoned executives, board members, funding sources, and advisers who will be able to tackle the decision making and paperwork required to drive an IPO effectively. No start-up should consider an IPO until they are sufficiently mature.

People often ask me about the special-purpose acquisition company (SPAC) and what I think about it. As a nonfinancial expert, I always decline to offer a view on this process. But I can offer one observation from watching many SPACs fail. The SPAC process makes it easier for companies to go public, and perhaps this might be inconsistent with the more natural process of waiting to embark on such a difficult path.

If you are in the process of IPO planning or execution, however, then you already know the importance of your legal staff and the investment banking partners you have chosen—or the investment banking team that your investors have chosen. I have heard one founder after another, especially the ones who are more technical, tell me that the IPO process is the most challenging, frustrating, and complex set of tasks that they have ever had to address.

An investment bank will buy up the shares in your company and then work the phones to peddle your stock to buyers. All those hours in the lab, all those hours helping customers, and all those hours worrying about payroll—and it all comes down to some brokers peddling your stock. You will either be happy with the result, or you will be miserable; there is probably not much in between.

The bottom line is that if you are considering an IPO, then first look at the team, and if you feel they can handle things, then fine. And recognize that your investors will certainly have a lot to say about this. But if you look at your team and sense that they might not be up to the task, or if you think that you are being rushed into a process you are uncomfortable with (perhaps a SPAC), then beware.

CASE STUDY: FORTINET

More than two decades ago, I needed a vendor to help revive an architecture that, on reflection, was one of the first network-based security setups ever conceived. Designed by several Bell Labs experts, including John Kevan, Dan Solero, and many others, the solution had been put together as a prototype for several large retail clients using an early firewall product from a tiny company in India that had stumbled onto a good network security design.

But we seemed to be their only customer, and I remember their founder calling me to explain that he was out of money. This did not bode well for our architecture—and before long, I was chatting with the principals of a fine company being organized at the time called Fortinet. After some discussion, the Fortinet team, led by Ken Xie and his brother Michael, delivered exactly what we needed—and the rest is history.

Enterprise teams began to depend regularly on their service providers for managed firewall access integrated into the multiprotocol label-switching (MPLS) fabric, and Fortinet began to grow. If you had to design a more perfect growth pattern, it would be hard to beat what Fortinet has done since those early days in the 2000s. Revenue was $123 million in 2006, $615 million by 2013, and $3.3 billion in 2023.

Year-over-year (YOY) growth during that time never dipped below 15 percent but, perhaps more important, never exceeded 36.32 percent. The result has been a steady compounding of revenue and growth, including the company's IPO in November 2009. I think that Fortinet would be the one company that seems to violate the laws of gravity in the sense that it truly seemed to have grown in a stable and predictable manner with a minimum of turbulence.

I once had dinner in New York with Ken Xie and I asked him how he accomplished this type of growth. His answer, as anyone who knows this fine CEO would expect, was modest. But he did point to measured YOY growth as a key aspect of the company's success. I would recommend to founders prone to saying that they are growing at 1,000 percent or some other unsubstantiated rate, to learn from Fortinet. Slow and steady seems to win the race.

One proud additional personal note for me is that Ken Xie was kind enough to write a short blurb for a textbook on cybersecurity that I wrote in 2011. I think the book sold more based on his back-cover endorsement than on all my work.

PART THREE

DECISIONS AND ACTIONS

7

HOW SHOULD YOU WORK WITH ANALYSTS?

I first became aware of Gartner around the mid- to late 1990s, when I noticed their Magic Quadrants floating around the emerging web. It was fun to look at how these quadrants were used to rate and rank commercial vendors with such abandon. The company just seemed to have no qualms about saying that widgets from ACME were so much better than ones from Consolidated. You could say what you wanted about Gartner, but those Magic Quadrants certainly took a stand.

It got a bit personal, however, when they would rate services that I had a hand in developing and delivering at AT&T. And while I respected John Pescatore, the security lead analyst at the time, with a background at the National Security Agency (NSA) and Entrust, I also don't remember more than a couple of short meetings with Pescatore or any other Gartner analyst during that period, and my notes don't reflect any such meetings.

Since 1985, I have managed every day of my life in thirty-minute increments. I plan each day the night before and make sure that I am prioritizing what is urgent over what is important. Executives in start-ups should have a similar routine. During coaching, people often ask about the most important asset in any organization, and

I respond that it is the collective time of the team members. Manage your time wisely.

Meetings with Gartner that were either on or not on my calendar are not really a big deal. I suspect the analysts were probably talking to other groups in the company. But it just struck me as odd at the time because I would have liked to add my two cents. It is not Gartner's fault that I was left out, really—but I had valuable insight into the strengths and weaknesses of our offer.

QUADRANTS AND WAVES

In my present role, I often run into corporate buyers who still pay attention to Gartner Magic Quadrants or the similar Forrester Waves, which are also used to rate and rank vendors. These buyers explain to our team that placement in these quadrants and waves is a local requirement to justify the purchase of some vendor's commercial solution. Just a mention from Gartner seems to legitimize the decision to buy from a vendor.

The Gartner and Forrester marketing teams have done an amazing job. Vendors feel like they have no choice but to do anything necessary to be mentioned in a market report or to be placed in a quadrant or wave. And what's especially interesting is that it is considered better to be in the loser's portion of these grids than to be left off completely.

This leads to the awkward situation where a vendor pays Gartner to be rated in the bottom left quadrant of a grid that includes the vendor's competitors being rated higher. It doesn't make sense, but Gartner and Forrester, each now massive public companies, have created profitable businesses where their customers have no choice but to spend with them. This is the definition of being well into a mass market.

The structure of a quadrant or wave—and I see little difference— is that some designated vendor subset of a given market is selected, usually based on a business plan established by the analyst group, to identify a so-called category. By "business plan," I mean that the analyst group solicits paid involvement in the program for a given vendor to be included. Iconic vendors in a given category might be given a pass. (You can't do a quadrant on soft drinks without Coke.)

These selected vendors, perhaps a dozen or so, agree to pay the larger analyst teams roughly $100,000 or more to be included. I understand that prices vary and that the analysts swear that many companies are included in their grids without payment. However, I suspect that one good quadrant can generate several million dollars for an analyst firm. If they do several hundred quadrants across all areas of business, you can calculate the nice revenue stream that emerges. It's a genius model, albeit one that clearly benefits the analyst group more than any other participant.

The actual quadrants and waves tend to rate in two dimensions—one focused (sort of) on the product and the other focused (sort of) on the company. What this means is that the analyst team combines everything it knows about the vendor into a scaled rating of the function and execution of the product or service, and the strategy and planning of the company—often referred to as their vision. Something similar to the grid in figure 7.1 emerges.

The placement of vendors into the four boxes within the larger box creates a grid onto which managers can make purchase decisions. The placement of ACME, for example, suggests that it would be a much better choice than, say, Fasting. If Fasting matches your own local purchase criteria requirements (e.g., low price, knowledge of your domain), however, then this quadrant placement is not useful.

If you are comparing Managed, which is rated a good product from a weak company, and Visionated, which is rated a good company with a weak product, then you have to make your own determination. The biggest challenge for buyers is when Advantaged (weak product from a weak company) is your present vendor. Your management and board might want to do some research,

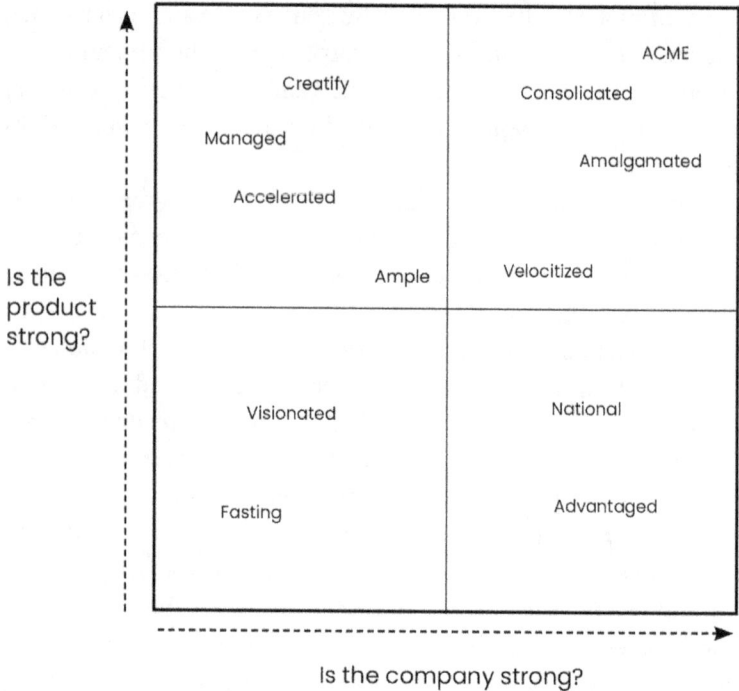

Figure 7.1 General structure of a quadrant or wave

which will probably result in you explaining that the quadrant was wrong.

In the end, every start-up will eventually have to deal with these quadrants and waves—not to mention other quantitative ratings from companies such as TAG (yes, we do this, too). The good news with ratings is that they are generally done for every company in an industry. At TAG, we rate almost 5,000 vendors in cybersecurity, and thousands more in AI and sustainability. This at least ensures that no one is left out of the process.

INDUSTRY ANALYSTS

The most commonly cited type of industry analyst focuses on financial returns and uses income statements, balance sheets, and other publicly available data to assess the financial performance of a company and to make predictions. This is almost always done in the context of public companies and offers guidance on whether a given stock will go up, down, or stay flat. Larger companies create analyst relations teams to manage these groups.

The type of industry analyst more applicable to a start-up, and the type exemplified by Gartner, Forrester, and TAG, has a different focus. Some observers call this type of analyst a "market analyst," but our preference is to use "industry analyst." The key point here is that we are not talking about analysts who suggest that you buy this stock over that one. That is irrelevant for start-ups.

What characterizes industry analysts is that they start with market trends from the perspective of different vendors and their respective buyers. Added to this is a focus on technology trends, specifically which way innovations seem to be addressed by different vendors. And finally are added industry-specific issues because the individuals we reference here are usually focused on specific domain areas.

As mentioned earlier, TAG works primarily in cybersecurity, but we have extended to other areas such as AI. In these areas of focus, we push out our subjective opinions, fully disclaimed by our lawyers. We do this to support best effort use by industry participants in their source selection decision making.

Industry analysts are like critics, so to speak. We will say that vendor A is the strongest in a given area and that vendors B, C, and D are . . . not so good. Like the producers of off-Broadway shows, your start-up team, working in the basement coding for your next cloud-based, mobility-enabled widget, will need good commentary from the analysts who matter.

HOW DO ANALYSTS MAKE MONEY?

This is the right question for any start-up to ask because under-standing this basic business fact about analysts helps founding teams and marketing executives in start-ups to better navigate the hazards that can emerge with analysts. The business model involves three things: influence, advice, and content. And the order matters in the relative importance and priority of how these benefits are accrued. Let's take them one at a time, starting with influence.

Industry analysts are fundamentally purveyors of influence—and this includes influence with buyers, sellers, regulators, innovators, researchers, observers, and any other stakeholders in a given indus-try. Such influence is typically provided through written reports, often called market reports, as opposed to other means (except at TAG, where social media, video, and even cartoons are considered important delivery mechanisms of influence.)

In its purest and most unbiased form, influence should be pro-vided by neutral yet informed observers who have no personal stake in whether good, bad, or indifferent reviews are given about a vendor or product. This influence, again in the purest sense, should be driven by a clear rubric, one that is transparent enough for anyone reviewing analyst reports to use as the basis for under-standing the analyst's thinking.

As you would expect, influence works best when it comes from organizations or individuals who carry some gravity in the domain of interest. A great solar panel product review from an analyst with a twenty-year professional background in the physics of photovol-taics carries more influence than a comparable review from a non-expert writer looking up terms on Google or on OpenAI.

Analyst firms, usually the larger ones, that drive influence through their logo tend to be the most biased unfortunately. In con-trast, analyst firms, usually the smaller boutique ones, that drive influence through their expert staff tend to be the least biased. This should come as no surprise because the latter group has its collective reputation on the line with every recommendation it make.

Gartner and Forrester are firms that use their logo to drive more biased influence, especially with senior leaders. They make their money—and a lot of it—by dishing out influence.

TAG is an example of a smaller analyst firm that uses high-profile people to drive influence. Dork Sahagian, for example, has worked as a TAG analyst, and he is a recognized world expert in climate-related science in addition to running the Lehigh University Environment Institute. When he likes something, you can be certain that his commentary will be entirely authentic.

The second component of an analyst firm's money-making machine involves advisory services. This is usually one of the more valuable offerings in the industry analyst portfolio. When done properly, these services involve a tailored learning journey in which customers are led through an introspective review of their beliefs ("why" statements), value propositions ("how" statements), and solution offerings ("what" statements).

Advisory services should be performed by experts with experience both in the target domain and in coaching from a curriculum. If an advisory relationship is set up in an unstructured, whatever-you-want-to-talk-about manner, then real discipline is required on both ends of the advisory sessions to maintain some semblance of progress, which is possible but not easy. And too many advisers take this route out of ignorance or, worse, incompetence.

I coach many start-up executives on both a weekly and monthly basis, and they constitute collectively a mix of structured and unstructured sessions. The book you are reading right now is influenced significantly by these sessions. If you look at the contents in the front of this book, you'll get an idea of how we proceed.

Our advice to start-ups is that, if they engage with an analyst firm, then they should specifically demand clarity regarding advisory sessions. If the sessions are limited in number and scope, and if you notice, as I have in the past, that your so-called expert knows less about the topic than you do and, worse, always seems to be talking to you from a sailboat, or airport, or restaurant, then save your money. ChatGPT will give you better answers to your questions.

The final aspect of analyst services involves content, which will vary in quality. Let's start with tailored content that was commissioned for a paying client. The types of content usually offered by analyst firms include technical reports on a platform or other solution; blogs written either as guest articles or coauthored pieces for a vendor; or return on investment (ROI) reports, which we examine in more detail later in this chapter.

Everyone will have a different view of what constitutes a quality piece of written content. I have delivered, for example, virtually the same technical report—common style, similar outline, comparable depth of technical information—to two different marketing teams in roughly the same market. And I have seen one group hail the report while the other returns it with an F on the cover. Content quality exists in the eye of the beholder.

As for published research content, this should, at least in theory, be the greatest perk involved in working for an analyst firm because it allows more freedom of analysis, expression, and interpretation. Published research varies greatly, however, because the larger analyst firms like Gartner are extremely careful in terms of messaging by their analysts in public settings. They will never publish anything that can cost them money with a client.

But this is true for any public company with billions in revenue at stake. As a result, analysts from the larger firms will write research reports with vacuous but noninflammatory statement like this: "We recommend that you develop requirements for IT management by defining the needs of your IT management relevant to the IT management considerations in use at your company."

That is a statement that will never result in the author being questioned—or sued. But it tends to be the smaller analyst firms, like TAG, who will be freer and more open with their subjective opinions, often expressing ideas that could anger even their own clients. This makes content from small analyst firms infinitely more interesting to read than that from the bigger teams.

Content can also be nonwritten. For example, most analyst firms have mastered the art of the webinar. These include the obligatory analyst who opines on the market, an expert from the start-up company paying for the webinar, and maybe a couple of practitioners who use the start-up's product. When done right, a webinar can be informative, but when done wrong, it can be a snoozefest for listeners.

Our advice at TAG regarding webinars designed to bring marketing attention to your start-up comes down to two things. First, pick topics that you are passionate about and make them detailed and specific to what you do. Second, pick participants who share that passion and who can speak for hours about what they love. In this manner, five people talking about needlepoint will be awesome listening for anyone passionate about needlepoint.

But you cannot fake real, and this also goes for video interviews by analysts. Your start-up interview with the fancy analyst should be an honest chance for you to share your passion with someone equally interested. If the interviewer and interviewee really, and I mean really, like the topic, then the result will be great for others of shared interest. The idea here is not to win an Emmy but to generate attention *and business* for your start-up.

WHAT IS PAY FOR PLAY?

This is an important enough topic to require its own section in this chapter—and it is something that every start-up founding team should understand. Pay for play is a quid-pro-quo situation in which an analyst firm adjusts the recommendations, opinions, and ratings it issues for a given vendor proportional to the amount of money that vendor pays. It is not an ethical practice, and it might even be considered fraudulent in some contexts.

For large companies, participating in pay for play is generally tolerated. The analyst relations team keeps an eye to ensure that the approach is not too egregious but generally remains quiet as long as their company is treated well in the ratings. But for start-ups, this can be a backbreaker, especially if the pay-for-play fees are high. Let's examine the subtleties a bit more.

First, I believe that it is 100 percent fine for an analyst firm to develop ratings as long as the process is transparent. I understand that pay for play has been challenged in court, and I'd say that if you want the definitive view on this topic, refer to the law and check with your lawyer. I am unaware of any lawsuit that has been successful in this regard. My advice is to forget about litigation and save your legal dollars for something else.

But you, the start-up buyer, should know how this works—and here is the subtlety. If an analyst firm gives you a D-minus based on a publicly available rubric and couched by all the proper language around it being their opinion, then it is also reasonable for them to offer consultation on how you might take steps to improve this rating. This is different from having them take money just to increase the rating. It's a subtle but important difference.

A second issue related to pay for play is that I believe it is acceptable for analyst firms to take money from vendors, but the practice should always include some sort of clear and tangible service rendered. If an analyst firm is developing written, video, or webinar content using experts, for example, then these are good cases of services rendered, and there is no reason why the analyst firm should not be compensated. At TAG, we call this "pay for work."

The nuance here is that, by working with a vendor, the analyst firm naturally becomes more knowledgeable about that vendor's solution. Based on this work, the analyst team is more likely to recommend them and even to (and I type the following words with extreme care) *rate them higher* than competing firms. Of course, if the work uncovers holes in a product, then the result could be the opposite.

This might sound like pay for play, but remember that all business involves one individual or group recommending products and services to another. It's how the business world has always worked. Where problems emerge is when analyst firms take the easy way out. As a start-up founder, be careful who you work with.

ROI ANALYSES

Whenever I read an ROI analysis that suggests that some product offers a 1,000 percent in-year return on the investment, I wonder about the implications of such a claim. Suppose that you commission Forrester to develop a total economic impact (TEI) calculation. Forrester will likely include in the calculation savings such as fewer hours worked, reduced insurance premiums, and other cost reductions. They do this because they want the ROI to be as high as possible.

One might presume that if an ROI of 100 percent is good, then a return of 200 percent is better, and an ROI of 300 percent is better still. Of course, as the ROI numbers get large, things can get a bit weird. A 300 percent ROI implies that if I spend $100 on ACME's product, I will see savings or some other benefit in the tangible amount of $300. The questionable ROI reports I have seen quantify this $300 using some mushy concept like reduced workload, or improved quality of work life, or something like that.

When you commission an ROI, you have two options: First, you can show that, by investing in your widget today, certain costs will be lower tomorrow. This is the take-vitamins-today-to-avoid-sickness-tomorrow argument. Second, you can show that, by investing in your low-cost ACME widget, you can toss out high-cost products from other vendors. This is the replace-your-expensive-gas-guzzler-with-my-electric-car argument.

Our coaching at TAG is to be conservative in laying out ROI analysis and to avoid specifically the common trap of trying to translate qualitative benefits into dollars. Suppose that an information technology (IT) team pays two staff members $100 per hour to do manual software patching. Let's also assume that they spend half of their time, or twenty hours per week on this work. You'd get this data, of course, from the IT managers during ROI preparation.

If you do the calculations, you can see that the IT team is spending about $200,000 per year on this manual work. Any reasonable observer would agree that automating this process would free up time for the two staff members. But it is unlikely that the two individuals would be fired. It is much more likely that they would be reassigned to do higher-value work. This would not result in any cost savings because they would remain on the payroll.

I understand that you would save on hiring other staff, avoid attrition, and so on. But that is the whole point: Be conservative in your ROI. Let the readers of your ROI see the value your solution will bring them in terms of both quantitative and qualitative benefits.

CASE STUDY: TAG CYBER-RATINGS

At TAG, we use ten factors to rate cybersecurity vendors. We do our best to establish a fair but preliminary rating for every vendor, and this rating is usually based on inquiries from our enterprise customers. Once this preliminary rating is completed, we contact the vendor and offer, for a very small fee, the chance to have us dig deeper into their solution to make sure we fully understand their value and to provide coaching on how they can improve. These are updated, certified rating results.

We see this as being especially useful for enterprise teams who would like a numeric assessment of our view of a given vendor. Yes, the assessment is subjective, but our analysts have decades of experience and expertise in reviewing the potential effectiveness of commercial cybersecurity vendors. Buyers who read our ratings understand that we are basically putting our names to the ratings.

The comparison factors include company stage, message efficacy, pace of innovation, vision and strategy, strength of management, strength of references, financial strength, ability to scale, product functionality, and infrastructure maturity. For each factor, our analysts follow a common grading rubric based on our understanding of the company and its commercial offerings.

None of this is perfect, but the analysis, which results in a real number score between 0.0 and 10.0 provides a means for our team to communicate its subjective opinion about a vendor. As you might expect, start-up founders really need to keep an eye on this process. One incorrect or misleading rating can cause a buyer to look elsewhere. So make sure you work with the analysts.

8

WHAT IS YOUR GO-TO-MARKET (GTM) PROCESS?

One of the most practical considerations we advise start-up leaders to think through carefully is what they actually are selling. This might seem like the most obvious thing, hardly worth mentioning, but we meet regularly with new companies that have a great idea and that have created awesome technology and that tell an inspiring story—but when we ask them what they actually sell, it is often not clear.

An example is the software development kit (SDK). If done properly, an SDK can be an essential product for a developer, often helping to fill gaps in their software life cycle or architecture. But SDKs can also be excuses for start-ups who have no idea how to package their work into a product. Instead, they combine software libraries, routines, and other resources into a hodgepodge that developers sort out on their own. This approach rarely works.

MANAGING PROTOTYPES

A related issue involves prototypes, and this is an especially intense problem with start-ups emerging from research or academic labs. For example, there are some amazing technologists in the Applied Physics Laboratory (APL) at the Johns Hopkins University (JHU). The Asymmetric Operations Group under Donna Gregg, in particular, has been a place where I've truly enjoyed my years of consulting interactions. That group is a national treasure for the United States.

I bring up this team because of the amazing prototypes created in the context of their work with the U.S. federal government. I have spent countless hours at their headquarters in Maryland watching world-class researchers demonstrate their work, usually presented in the context of a prototype for a government sponsor. It's always an exhilarating experience because their work is often years ahead of what I see commercially.

The problem, however, is that, while prototypes are a great start, most products succeed or fail based on the support, interfaces, documentation, integrations, partnerships, and other business factors driven by product management teams. Customers do not buy prototypes. They buy products. And this causes many fine researchers to depart national labs in search of that Holy Grail of developing a product that customers will actually use.

As a result, I tell start-ups that they need to establish utter clarity around the specific products and services that they use to generate revenue. These products and services cannot be jumbles of things thrown together, nor can they be prototypes. They need to be fully defined and properly supported products. At the risk of sounding critical of the scientists or developers, I would say that the prototype is usually the easiest part of the product development process.

Salespeople are the truth tellers with respect to whether your products and services are defined correctly because, without clarity around the actual products and services being sold, there will be no revenue. When we hear that a start-up is having trouble keeping their sales teams in place, we usually ask to see the roster of what is actually for sale rather than review the sales process or compensation plans. What are the products? Answering this question is often the problem.

DO YOU HAVE A BUSINESS PLAN?

This is another obvious question, but it often leads to silence among start-up founders when it is asked. Or the founders will show us a PowerPoint presentation that explains the company vision, the customer base, the solutions addressed, the expected financials, and so on. And it is true that business plans must include financial plans, growth plans, product evolution plans, competitive plans, and so on.

I usually find that it is best to review these business plans in the context of the start-up's go-to-market (GTM) approach. Our view is that GTM plans for individual products or services should link to a higher-level business plan for the company. Your business plan should guide the company, and your GTM plans (plural) should guide introduction of your products and services, usually under the guidance of a product manager (discussed later in this chapter).

I can share a couple of observations about business plans, and while I don't think either one is a hard-and-fast rule, they show up often. The first is that, if you are working with a venture capital team or teams, then you will have a board with specific demands regarding your business plan. They will make it clear to you what they want to see, and you will often have little choice but to accept their guidance and business planning terms.

Some of the larger venture capital teams have working groups within their portfolio companies that review each other's business plans, and this is a good idea. Expect very specific guidance on what must be included in your business plan if you have external funding. This is something you can count on, and it is something you should welcome if you have selected a good venture partner with strong resources.

A second observation is that the best business plans link directly to clearly defined objectives, often in the context of quantified metrics. It is better to define your plan with specific numbers attached to tasks and initiatives than to keep things more qualitative. Rather than include a step that will "increase sales," it is infinitely better to target something like "improving our response rate to outbound emails 2 to 3 percent."

This is true for all aspects of your start-up business plan, which is most often done as a colorful PowerPoint deck. Each of the tasks and initiatives should be consistent with guidance from your funding source and include clearly defined quantitative goals that provide a useful target and context for your work. By developing plans in this manner, you will have a much better idea of how you are doing.

DO YOU HAVE A MARKETING STRATEGY?

Here is another question that is easy to ask but difficult to answer. Many early-stage start-ups respond that they cannot afford a marketing team and that, no, they do not have a marketing strategy. More mature start-ups approaching the chasm have either started with a marketing VP or taken the full plunge with a chief marketing officer (CMO). Those are the three stages: no marketing, VP-led, or CMO-led.

Business schools offer stilted definitions of marketing and associated strategies and, depending on how your mind works, such academic statements might not be useful. The most common marketing definition we see is roughly this: Marketing involves all the activity and processes that you must engage in to create, communicate, and deliver products or services with value for customers, clients, and other stakeholders.

Does that clear things up for you? In our estimation, start-ups find such vague notions of marketing to be basically useless. Instead, they eventually discover marketing in the context of the following tasks: outbound marketing to develop leads, inbound marketing to collect leads, outbound messaging based on content including social media, and development of sales materials and collateral to support briefings and events.

For start-ups flush with series A or later funding rounds, quite a bit of money is spent on these tasks, but so many mistakes are made in the execution of these tasks. Let's take some time below to examine our guidance related to start-up marketing. We hope that we can offer something that will either save you money or improve your results. And I hope that this guidance will also be applicable to teams in all stages of marketing maturity.

CUSTOMER SEGMENTATION

We are always surprised that customer segmentation is such an immature process for start-ups. Most new vendors instead show us a standard deck that tells the company and product story in a uniform manner. We might see a nuanced version with detailed financials used for fund raising or board meetings, or for meetings with analysts like us. But usually there is just this one uniform deck produced by the marketing team or founder.

As we have alluded to throughout this book such uniformity of approach is a mistake. Tailoring your marketing materials based on a segmented view of your customer base will do a better job of connecting your solution to actual interests and tribal traits. If this is not yet clear, then review chapter 3, where we include our recommendations for better understanding your customers.

In this chapter, let's discuss how you connect segmentation with your marketing tasks, namely, outbound lead generation, collection of inbound leads, outbound messaging, and sales collateral development. If you do an online search for the term "customer segmentation," then you will see a lot of nonsense about firmographics, demographics, product usage, and the like. Please ignore this academic mumbo-jumbo. Let me share instead a more realistic and practical business-to-business (B2B) segmentation strategy for a start-up.

The first customer segment, as shown in figure 8.1, is the founding team's network, which includes connections from previous jobs, close friends, family members, and colleagues. They exhibit

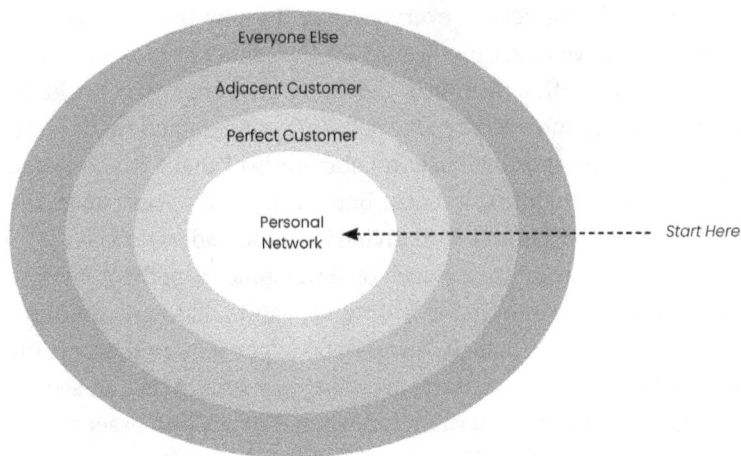

Figure 8.1 Early-stage start-up customer segmentation

varying demographics related to the size, scope, and focus of their organizations, but start-up founders should pay no mind. This personal network segment will get a start-up off the ground. It should be the top priority, in my estimation.

The second segment includes those buyers who match the vision the founders had in mind when they started the company. These are the so-called perfect customers, and investors often refer to these as ideal customer profiles or ICPs. For example, if you are selling online discovery tools for lawyers, then this group includes lawyers who need such tools. If you are selling a cloud-based supplier management system, then this group includes teams that manage suppliers.

The third segment includes so-called adjacent customers. These are the almost-perfect customers, except that they exhibit some characteristic that might not match 100 percent with the founding team's intent. Maybe the buyer is in a remote country, or is smaller than is ideal, or already has the type of widget you are selling. Usually, this segment demands slight tailoring of your solution.

The fourth segment is everyone else. I know this sounds a bit loose, but I have never met a start-up that didn't at least entertain any and every offer from any and every customer who might be requesting any and every type of solution. I understand that a start-up must focus, and obviously no start-up will make it across the chasm with a shotgun approach. But it is unwise to turn away any potential deal without at least giving it due consideration.

Start-ups in the latter stages of development, perhaps beyond the chasm and pondering exit options, can include an additional segment to the mix, namely, buyers who might acquire the start-up. This is only relevant for start-ups selling something that an acquiring entity might actually want, but when it is put into practice, the results can be exciting. What better way to demonstrate your success for an acquirer than to have them as a happy customer?

Notice that the marketing tasks are greatly simplified when we consider these four customer segmentation bubbles. For example, attention to outbound leads, inbound leads, outbound messaging, and sales collateral is significantly streamlined when we are talking about a founding team's personal network. They will need none of these marketing items. Instead, they just need a phone call, and a CMO is not needed for that.

When targeting the ICP segment, notice that the purpose of all four tasks is to help the buyer understand how perfect they are for the start-up's offering. It's a matter of holding up a mirror and showing the champion and approver that the start-up company was literally developed with them in mind. Every aspect of the marketing program should focus on this we-are-perfect-for-each-other approach.

For the adjacent customer segment, the purpose of marketing should be to demonstrate the flexibility and tailoring that can be done to help an almost-perfect customer become a perfect customer. This can be extended to the everyone-else segment, but start-ups would be wise to avoid shotgun marketing in lieu of sticking with more wheelhouse groups, beginning with the founder's network, which can be substantial in some cases.

INDUSTRY CONFERENCES

When I ask start-up founding teams about how things went at some recent industry conference, their answer is always some combination of amazing and stupendous. I love conferences, despite souring on their business value in recent years (I'll explain). When founders and marketing teams tell me that their conference booth was so busy that the lines were out the door, this response is expected.

I mention this because 100 percent of start-up founders will not be dissuaded from spending the money to grab a booth or at least a hotel suite at industry events applicable to their solution. In cybersecurity, the major conferences are the RSA Conference in San Francisco, California, in April, and the Black Hat Conference in Las Vegas, Nevada, in August.

At these conferences, start-ups and other vendors pay for travel and accommodations for team members. They pay for registration at the conference for all team attendees. They pay for the conference booth, which can be expensive. They pay for dinners with clients, food and drinks in reception suites at your hotel, swag and reports to be provided as handouts to attendees. And they pay for sponsored talks by your product and technical staff.

For early-stage start-ups, the total amount spent can often approach what it might cost to hire a software developer for a year. For larger start-ups, the total amount can grow to what it might cost to hire a small team of staff for a year. Think about that: Three days in a convention hall is viewed as comparable in value to hiring new team members who will contribute to your company every day.

I am not going tell you, nor do we do so in our coaching at TAG, that you should stay away from industry events. Instead, we recommend that you set your objectives with razorlike focus on obtaining contacts, period. I spent decades in a massive company with unlimited resources, and we could use major conferences as a training and even staff retention tool. But for start-ups, this is an expensive practice.

Here is what I advise start-ups regarding industry events, conferences, and other gatherings. First, we are highly suspicious of the return on investment (ROI) for large events. Marketing experts generally use these events to maintain their own career prospects, so they are incentivized to show positive ROI. But they are usually comparing contacts and leads gathered against a week of doing nothing versus comparing it against a week of hard inbound and outbound work.

Second, I am a proponent of start-ups getting involved in free local events with universities and industry groups. In cybersecurity and other disciplines, there are industry alliances that vendors are welcome to support, perhaps by buying lunch for a local meeting. We see these events as well-suited to start-ups. They can also create long-term relationships with students who might carry their goodwill to their first industry positions.

Third, I recommend that you be very careful with paid events such as speed-dating sessions where you pay to meet prospects. A less expensive approach might be to list your top prospects and invite them to give a lunch-and-learn talk to your team. Or you might ask permission to include a link on your website to some talk or article that they have published. These require more legwork, but when they work, they really work.

MARKETING A START-UP BRAND

If you invest in marketing, then please do so in light of the segmentation guidance we presented earlier in this chapter. Your initial customers will come from your network, and these buyers do not need brochures. They need personal outreach and concierge attention, which implies that marketing teams should be much more focused on connecting with perfect and adjacent customers and, as we explained earlier, innovators and early adopters connect based on belief systems.

Most marketing staff in start-ups have a lot of trouble accepting this basic fact. They prefer to design a complex playbook that highlights product features and showcases functional advantages. They align themselves two inches from the product, so to speak, but our guidance is that they should be viewing things 50,000 away from the product. And they would be wise to do this by deciding how to market the start-up's brand.

This task of brand definition for a start-up is easier to demonstrate than to define. For big companies like Apple, this business of disrupting the status quo and thinking differently all looks so easy. But for start-ups, such branding is not easy. It is necessary, however, because reaching the chasm demands innovators and disrupters. The more product-oriented marketing becomes more critical at and beyond the chasm. To get there, you need a brand.

CASE STUDY: FORTRA

Our team at TAG is always so pleased when our start-up clients graduate to an initial public offering (IPO) or acquisition by a larger entity. Agari, for example was an excellent start-up founded by my friend Pat Peterson, who is an expert and pioneer in email security. Peterson was literally the second person to write a check to my company after I set it up. We worked with Agari for almost six years, until they were purchased by a large company called HelpSystems.

When Peterson told me about the transaction, I had never heard of HelpSystems. But then suddenly, they hit my radar screen hard. Another longtime client of ours, Digital Defense, run by another loyal customer, Larry Hurtado, was also purchased by HelpSystems. And then Tripwire (a prior customer for two years), Digital Guardian (a prior customer for one year), and other interesting start-ups were being acquired by this interesting and possibly unusual company.

I should explain my use of the word "unusual" because this is not the typical, high-flying, cybersecurity-acquiring entity. Instead of being in Palo Alto, California, for example, HelpSystems is located in Minneapolis, Minnesota. And instead of being built through high finance and big funding, HelpSystems grew by supporting information technology (IT) and mainframe customers. And they were profitable. The problem is that no one in security knew HelpSystems. They had no brand.

We had the privilege to begin engaging with HelpSystems as they rebranded the company as Fortra. They engaged TAG to do an original series of content as they introduced themselves as a trusted partner, outside the fast-talking nonsense one finds so often in Silicon Valley. They presented themselves as collection of diamond-in-the-rough start-ups who now work better together than as separate entities. It's a wonderful brand story.

CASE STUDY: HUMAN SECURITY

Human Security, founded by the charismatic Tamer Hassan (now executive chair of the company), has been a consistent leader in fighting those bots that are the scourge of the internet. Human Security was a TAG customer for years, and I've interviewed their executives in my New York office on multiple occasions. Hassan was featured prominently in *Fast Company* magazine (as was TAG, by the way), and the company was recently listed as one of the one hundred most influential companies by *Time* magazine.

Much of this is driven by a capable executive team that has guided Human Security's growth during its trek toward and over the chasm. (Human Security has had marketing team members who I suspect could easily have written this chapter.) Although Human Security makes their business look easy, that was not always the case. In 2020, the company had a challenge, and it had to do with their name at the time: WhiteOps.

Anyone in cybersecurity knows that we routinely referred to malicious actions by hackers or criminals as black operations, black hat methods, and so on. We referred to defensive tasks by companies and agencies as white operations, white hat methods, and so on. This was the norm at the time, but I can see how the interpretation of the words, phrases, and references we use each day in society has changed, and for the better.

As you would expect, some companies might have ignored the naming conflict and perhaps relied on the fact that their brand linked to well-defined concepts. And I also suspect that none of Human Security's customers complained. But the management team decided to rename and rebrand the company. When I first heard of this plan, I shuddered at the complexity of the task and its many ripple effects across content, documentation, and so on.

After considerable research, and we were pleased at TAG to have participated in this step, the company decided on Human Security— or just Human. This was a bold decision because the word "human" is well represented in terms of search engine optimization (SEO). When you search for the term on the internet, for example, you are treated to information on Homo sapiens and the like.

But the renaming worked well, and Human Security is now referenced as one of the more creative brands in cybersecurity, perhaps as close to Apple in their "think different" approach to cyber as one will find. It's a master class in demonstrating good social awareness while also having the courage to make a risky change. I believe that the renaming worked because the underlying belief system at Human Security never shifted. To me, that is the key.

GTM STRATEGY

GTM strategies for start-ups come in two varieties: the big splash and the soft launch. If you ask which approach is better, my answer—and the answer of our entire TAG analyst team—would be, "It depends." We've reviewed enough GTM plans, strategies, tactics, and road maps to know that no single GTM formula applies generally. Every product launch is different because the products, buyers, context, and timing will be different.

The good news is that I can share some GTM heuristics that have been helpful to start-ups. For example, when start-ups recognize that their competition, whether direct, indirect, symmetric, or asymmetric, cannot easily duplicate what's being launched, then a big splash is best. Proclaiming boldly and loudly that you have something truly new is an awesome approach if competing forces can only sit and watch.

Take the ChatGPT launch in late 2022. That product made it faster to 1 million users than anything that had ever preceded it. A soft controlled launch, perhaps to some test customers, would not have been as effective. It might have given Google the time to see what was happening and develop a competing deployment plan. Instead, Google was forced to rush a response and their GenAI demo was a disaster. (They eventually got it right, of course.)

An additional heuristic in creating a GTM strategy plan is the amount of product that will be made available for purchase. Recognize that some of the most successful products are designed to be provided for limited use. Harvard University, for example, is hardly a start-up, but they clearly limit acceptance rates to drive higher levels of exclusivity. Luxury brands like Louis Vuitton execute this GTM play perfectly.

But this is not always the right approach. Imagine, for example, if Microsoft had allowed only a select number of exclusive customers to use Microsoft 365. The massive and explosive growth of that capability probably would not have happened. Apple's virtual reality helmet (which most of us have already forgotten) was an interesting GTM example. With a price tag of over $3,000, they limited the number of buyers and, by most accounts, the product was a flop, which is unusual for Apple.

One heuristic that seems true for both the big splash and the soft launch is the importance of creating anticipation in GTM planning. This is not easy for a start-up because customers might not know you, your team, or your product. Anticipation and industry buzz can nevertheless be generated, and social media, especially LinkedIn, is a wonderful vehicle. LinkedIn has become the watercooler for global business and, if you are clever, you can attract attention.

At TAG, we do this with our cartoon series called *Charlie CISO*. We do a new cartoon every week, and we do not skimp on the talent. We use a professional cartoonist, Rich Powell, as our artistic and creative superpower. I can't tell you how much attention our cartoons have generated and how successful they have been at generating awareness of our messaging. (We once developed a commissioned cartoon for Secretary of State Madeline Albright before she passed.)

Video works well, too, and if you create interesting content that is easy to understand, covers interesting topics, and is produced creatively, then you can attract attention and create anticipation for your product. Be careful with podcasts, however, because they demand the sensibility of an entertainer who is willing to be open, vulnerable, and honest with an audience. Snoozefest podcasts that tout your product in safe corporate-speak are a waste of time. We live in an era of podcasts—so if you are not going to be honest and open, then stay away from this medium.

The next GTM heuristic sometimes gets me in trouble, but I will say it anyway: I know that public relations (PR) companies can be enticing, but they can also be a massive waste of money. You can write your own press releases—in fact, ChatGPT does a marvelous job of generating perfectly acceptable copy. And if you want to connect with reporters, then for heaven's sake, connect with them on LinkedIn.

I bet you will find that many of the better reporters in your field have a surprisingly small number of connections and followers on LinkedIn. Join and be noisy. Take the time to like their posts and comment on their articles. Get them to notice you, and I suspect that they will take an interest in figuring out who you are. This is not conjecture, by the way: I have seen this done to great effect.

Finally, create, post, and share good content when you can. If you cannot do it yourself, then hire some company, freelancer, or intern to help you generate an ongoing stream of content. It could be blogs, articles, commentary, posts, reports, and so on. I'm not talking about reposts; I am talking about you and your start-up team creating original content.

Nothing, and I mean nothing, is more powerful than generating something interesting that others read. They learn about you and your company, and you might even find that you like doing it. For start-up GTM strategies, content is the oil that lubes the engine.

CASE STUDY: THE SEGWAY

An interesting case study in GTM strategy involves the Segway, a two-wheel product that was about as anticipated back in the 2000s as one could ever imagine. The general view at the time was that the Segway product would fundamentally change transportation, especially in cities. Major hype was emerging from well-known people such as Dean Kamen, the rich inventor of the device, as well as from Jeff Bezos of Amazon, Steve Jobs of Apple, John Doerr of Kleiner Perkins, and others.

When the product was launched in 2001, the argument could be made that the transport vehicle could barely live up to its high expectations. The company opted for a soft launch rather than a big splash, which was what Jobs had recommended. Only police departments, recreation parks, and other groups had access to the vehicle initially, which cut out a large portion, the biggest portion, of the potential market.

Aside from some battery problems and high costs, the product soon emerged as a safety hazard. One accident after another started to hamstring the company. Famous people like President George W. Bush and others fell off the device in front of the media, and it became obvious that there really were some safety issues. The company even sold itself to a billionaire named James Hazelton who *died* while riding a Segway when he went off a cliff.

The product started to look utterly ridiculous, and its brand, image, and reputation are now evocative of some nerdy person riding it. In retrospect, the Segway marketing team might have launched the product with a big splash at a lower cost to a wider audience. They could have focused on safety, perhaps providing lots of resources, training, and information on safe riding. And they could have worked on the image, perhaps paying high-profile individuals to use the device. Instead, the company got film character Paul Blart, the mall cop, as their unintended visual spokesperson.

Today, students of marketing in business schools around the world review the Segway case study in the classroom to better understand exactly what not to do during a GTM start-up launch.

PRODUCT MANAGERS

An important position in a start-up is the product manager. For nearly a century, companies such as Proctor & Gamble had product managers known as brand men. But Procter & Gamble is hardly a start-up company. Some connect the start-up product manager role with Hewlett Packard (HP), whose founders, William Hewlett and David Packard, apparently pioneered the use of product managers in their start-up company.

Modern start-ups almost always include the role of a product manager. For software companies, the introduction of rapid and agile software development had a lot to do with the need for such a position. Software products, and frankly just about every other start-up offering imaginable, are now developed so quickly that it's hard to connect things like features, versions, and releases with the demands and requests actually originating with customers.

Companies once could design a product using research and instinct and then deliver it to customers. As the cycle from design to delivery began to shorten, especially for software, a new process emerged in which an early version of a product is introduced and provided to customers for early feedback. This is then incorporated into enhancements to the product, which is then relaunched for feedback, and so on.

Software people call this iterative process DevOps, and a new position, the product manager, was needed to manage the process between the developers and the customers. In other industries, the same term is used for comparable roles. The best product managers are advocates for the customers and serve as the liaison between product developers and users.

The skills required to be a good product manager are considerable, and start-ups should be very careful when choosing someone to perform this task. A good product manager must be technical, and this can be a challenge when the perception exists that a good developer or otherwise technical person agrees either to step down or to sell out to become a product manager.

Start-up founders should work hard to ensure that product managers are considered an essential part of the product development community, and any substantive activities such as technology training or decisions about people to include in developer meetings should be carefully considered to include the product manager. Details like who is invited to meetings can go a long way toward supporting or destroying relationships in a start-up.

Good product managers must understand what customers want and need. This is not something that can be easily taught, unfortunately, for the same reason that you cannot teach empathy. And with product managers, the need to understand customers and to serve as the customer advocate is not easy to teach. We tell start-up founders to stay close to their product managers because their role and function are that important.

9

HOW DO YOU SELL?

Let's start with a personal challenge I have seen with many start-ups: They often fail to understand that their most important collective task is to sell. When asked about their top priorities, they often share references to strategy, attracting good people, delivering a great product, and so on. All are obviously important tasks.

But if a start-up wants to grow, the number one priority must be sales. The start-up needs to establish healthy sales to excellent paying customers. Money must be flowing from the customers' bank accounts to yours. That must be the priority because everything else is just window dressing.

When founders, especially those with technical backgrounds, are uncomfortable with this fact, it reduces their chances of growth. Every principal in a successful start-up must learn to obsess about sales, and this requires having the courage to ask for business. Start-up teams must be willing to go face-to-face with customers and ask them for their business.

Here are some statements that should flow from the mouths of start-up team principals as freely as ordering lunch: "Can I count on your business?" "Can I send you a contract?" "Shall I sign you up today?" "When can we arrange to begin our proof of concept?"

"Where do I send the paperwork?" "How many licenses can I put you down for?"

Some founders find it easy to ask such questions. They are comfortable with the idea that selling involves solving problems for customers. They can convince themselves that the customer would be better off having the solution being pitched than if they just kept their money or used it for a competing solution. Great sales cultures nurture this belief.

While this approach correctly focuses on the needs of customers, even the best start-ups can also turn their attention inward. When they do this, they quickly understand that without sales, there is no company.

In this chapter, we outline a series of ideas and tips that have arisen in our work from various means, including time spent coaching start-ups, my personal experience selling, and all sorts of interesting advice that I've collected over the years from many wonderful sales resources—both new and old. For example, my favorite book of all time about sales is Frank Bettger's *How I Raised Myself from Failure to Success in Selling*, published more than eight decades ago. Several of his ideas are transposed into the guidance in this chapter.

WHO SHOULD BE IN CHARGE OF SELLING?

I have observed that far too many start-ups view selling as a process that is assigned to a sales leader and that when things do not go as planned (that is, they experience poor sales), the solution is to find a new sales leader.

Here is some advice that would be impossible for me to underemphasize: Successful start-ups do not assign their sales to an individual or group. Selling is part of the culture, and this must begin at the top with the founder and founding team members. Without sales, you have no company.

It is perfectly reasonable for a start-up company to hire a good sales leader to coordinate the overall process of how to engage customers, solicit meetings, close deals, run product pitches, and measure success. This is fine, and I suspect that any new company with venture capital funding already knows this.

We love to have teams of eager sales development representatives (SDRs) working together with account executives and sales leaders to maximize inbounds from prospects and to flood the zone with outreach, content, and social media posts. SDRs are requirements, but they are hardly sufficient to drive a culture of selling.

If you have influence over the culture at your start-up, then I hope you will commit to making it clear that sales is the responsibility of every employee. For example, sales referrals should come in constantly from team members, and they should be celebrated and even compensated. In addition, sales calls might routinely include staff from the development team, or finance, or other aspects of the company so that they can listen to a real conversation with a live prospect.

Everyone must understand that selling is the lifeblood. It is the air your company breathes. Without sales, you go out of business.

UNDERSTANDING YOUR CONTRACTS

One topic that is underrepresented in popular books, articles, and courses on general selling is contracts. When we ask start-up team members, which often include sales vice presidents, to explain their sales contracts, it is not unusual for them to share a rather vague response. When we ask to review their contracts, we are often sent multiple files with unclear titles and no guide for how to read them. The contract documents often look like they were created by someone with ChatGPT and a legal dictionary.

It's common for start-up contracts to have the usual clauses that explain what's being sold, terms of use, certain payment expectations, and so on. But when we ask about or point to some simple item in the contract, many salespersons will shrug and admit that they are not exactly certain what it means. This is a massive mistake, if only because you are asking a customer to sign a document that you do not even understand.

It should be reinforced that when I say "understand" in this context, I mean really understand the contract. This means being able to explain it confidently to someone who knows nothing about contracts, and that usually means your influencer buyer. We say this because approver buyers usually have more knowledge of contracts than influence buyers.

I know many readers might be thinking that many customers do not read contracts. They leave them for procurement, legal, and contract staff to iron out. I admit that this can be true, but even when you work with procurement staff in a business-to-business (B2B) context to work out the details of some contractual point, they will eventually bring in the actual buyer.

Our belief is that when a sales professional takes the time to learn the details of a contract, they are showing respect for their customer. They are acting as the customer advocate to make sure that every clause is reasonable. If the salesperson were to be presented with the contract as a buyer, then they would be personally comfortable signing it.

Learning the details of your contract is a show of respect for your customer. It's a vital point to keep in mind.

I understand that this is unconventional advice because so many sales trainers (and I've had several) recommend not wasting time on the contractual boiler plate. But I think this is a mistake. Your contract is the formal interface with your customer, and you should know what each sentence and clause means. Take the time to learn all of them, and you will see improved sales results.

USE CUSTOMER RELATIONSHIP MANAGEMENT (CRM) AS A TOOL, NOT A GOAL

Using customer relationship management (CRM) tools for sales is essentially a given for any start-up with the usual leads, prospects, active negotiations, and paying clients. There is simply no justification for tracking important sales metrics manually—unless you are a tiny, pre-revenue start-up with only a few contacts outside the company. I did this work manually, for example, during the first three years of our existence at TAG.

But for everyone else, and this implies pretty much every start-up, your sales team will need CRM, and the big kahuna in this business is Salesforce. They provide the most feature-rich offering, and most sales professionals have experience with this software-as-a-service (SaaS) tool. There are cheaper options, such as HubSpot or Pipedrive.

If you have some reasonable tool in place, use it realistically. The mistake we have often observed being made by sales professionals in start-ups involves using CRM-related metrics as actual goals rather than as tools toward the real goal, which is sales. Do not let CRM updates mistakenly become the goal rather than the means.

Many start-up sales teams also decide that closing deals requires doing more demos. They therefore incentivize sales teams to meet a demo target, perhaps ten per week. This can lead to the awkward situation where a customer has already agreed to a deal, but the sales engineer will insist on doing a demo. If the demo goes well, fine. But if it goes badly, then you could lose the business.

Here's an example of a sales incentive at work. Gartner has a salesperson who calls on me from time to time. She knows that I would not buy from Gartner, but she is happy to do a demo for me when she needs an additional completed discussion and demo to meet her quota. I am happy to listen and learn the latest, while she goes plus-one on her demo target. The arrangement seems like a total win-win to me.

CREATE HONEST SALES METRICS

Being an analyst implies that you deal with metrics constantly, and you come to appreciate quickly how metrics must provide proper insight in the correct context. While I was in graduate school, I first became aware of an amazing book called *How to Lie with Statistics*, by Darrell Huff, which was my first exposure to the idea that someone might intentionally manipulate metrics to divert attention from some uncomfortable issue.

Today, we take for granted that an organization might twist a graph, trend, matrix, or other structure to support a predefined conclusion. This is really using metrics backward; that is, you arrive at a conclusion first and then shape some narrative using metrics and numbers that were selected and trimmed to support your points.

If an opinion commentator does this on TV, let's hope that we all have the good sense to see through the façade. But if you do this to manage your start-up, especially with respect to sales or financial trends, then you are flirting with disaster. And by "disaster," I mean not making payroll or even losing your company. Start-ups must be honest in the metrics they select and the data they provide to populate such metrics.

Suppose your monthly sales target is $500, 000. This would make you a $6 million company, which is common in the seed to series A stage of growth for a start-up. You will inevitably review your expenses carefully and if you have venture capital funding, then you will be asked to set your monthly payroll, rent, and other operating expenses at a number higher than $500,000 per month. The goal, of course, is to push for hypergrowth.

The negative difference between take and spend is known as burn rate, and if you lie to yourself about this number, then you can and will lose your company. The implication, obviously, is that every metric you select for your start-up should be carefully considered and then used in a manner that accepts only those data that are valid and perhaps overly conservative.

Take some time with your team and develop an honest dashboard. If you have venture capital funding, then the principals will have demanded such action. But for other start-up founders, it is imperative that you create an honest set of metrics that provide exactly the right insight into how well (or not) you are doing. In the context of sales, these metrics should be quantitative and focused on deals, signed contracts, and revenue.

OBSESS ABOUT SALES LEADS

The image of the annoying insurance salesperson working the rounds at a cocktail party, incessantly soliciting everyone for business is cliché. If you are running a start-up or if you sell for one, however, then I am sorry to report that you must be, or you must at least approximate, that solicitous insurance salesperson. This might not be great for your social life, but you handed in that card when you agreed to the start-up life.

Obsessing on leads does not require that you be annoying, but it does dictate that you be ravenous when it comes to identifying sales leads for your start-up. This can be a serious personal challenge for many founders, especially those who come from domain-specific disciplines such as engineering or software development. These folks often developed their domain skills while disliking (even hating) sales. The irony is that once these experts start or join a start-up, they must rethink this belief system. In many cases, they must embrace the thing they once despised.

This does not always work, however. For example, in some start-ups, the technical founder might decide that they are too busy for sales. This is obviously nonsense.

My advice to anyone working in a start-up whose founders say that they are too busy for sales would be to find another job. As a corollary, when a founding team says that sales just happen and that inbounds arrive without the need to do any active solicitation, I'd also advise quitting. Sales might just happen over a short period of time, but believing this will always be the case results in bad habits. Sales must be actively engaged. They do not just happen.

Running a successful start-up demands a sales culture, and this is true for all employees supporting all levels of products, platforms, services, technology, and so on. As we stated at the beginning of this chapter, without sales, there is no business, and only one-in-a-million companies hang their shingle to the delight of customers coming unsolicited. As I have said, unsolicited sales do not just come.

This issue can be confusing if they watched OpenAI's deployment of ChatGPT, which did not require obsessive sales solicitation. At TAG, we plead with our clients to ignore these misleading cases. Your product will not exhibit the same inbound demand as ChatGPT. Your chances of rolling out a product that customers will beg for without you developing leads is about as likely as you winning the lottery. If you decide to avoid building a sales solicitous culture, one where everyone, including family, friends, colleagues, associates, and acquaintances, is a potential customer, then you are basically banking on winning the lottery. This issue of obsessing about sales is worth repeating in your mind over and over: To reach the chasm with a new start-up, you must sell, sell, and sell like your life depended on it. And for some founders, it does.

PERSONALIZE COMMUNICATIONS

I have spent a lifetime working in cybersecurity. One of our industry goals is to solve the spam problem. We do so not from the perspective of wanting to restrict people's ability to communicate but rather to reduce the chances of people getting a phishing or malware-laden email. In addition to creating security risk, these emails call into question the integrity of every inbound message that comes across your screen.

It is reasonable to say that spam has rendered unsolicited email as mostly junk. In the early days of email, this was not the case. The movie *You've Got Mail* (1998) has a title that references the old AOL notification that an email has arrived, as if this were an event to be celebrated and as if that would be anything other than the most mundane and repetitive thing in your life.

The typical businessperson today receives literally hundreds of emails in their inbox every day. When you write an email to your customer, prospect, lead, partner, supplier, or whomever, your message will be viewed (often in preview mode) next to 100 other such email previews that come in every day.

I tell start-up clients to find some means for personalizing their communications with prospects, leads, and clients. This is hard work, and it demands that you allocate hours to tasks that might otherwise take minutes. You can and should personalize communications to partners and suppliers, although it is admittedly less important for sales success. It's just a good way to do business.

For email, personalization means never writing anything that smacks of mass-generated spam, and you know exactly what I mean. Spam is the email that includes proclamations about how great a product is, usually in a bold font, and that refers to the recipient of the email generically. These notes scream spam, and your eye has learned to spot them.

If you and your SDRs take this generic route to save time and money or, worse, if you are paying interns to create these emails, then please stop because it will not work. If you must write an email, then write it briefly so that it looks as though you're dashing off something to a close colleague. Keep it really simple and personalize the note; reference something about the recipient—as we illustrate in figure 9.1.

I know this does not scale, and I know that it prevents you from blasting out the email from your CRM to thousands of leads. But our experience working with start-ups is that twenty carefully crafted and personalized notes from the inbox of the founder work better than 20,000 spam emails from the inbox of an intern. And this is a wonderful metric to track on your sales dashboard.

It is true that personalizing communications doesn't scale, but no one promised that running a start-up was going to be easy.

Hello Edward,

Is your team at TAG INC. trying to save money on software development costs? One of the largest companies in the world reports that the **revolutionary** ACME AI Coding Platform saved them a staggering $90M in development costs. They have 19,000 employees across 300 offices.

Would you like to attend our customer panel session at the upcoming AI Developers Conference in Orlando? You can sign up **here** to attend.

Another Fortune 50 customer proclaimed this the year of AI Coding - and ACME has been working with this large company to improve their applications and reduce costs.

YOU TOO can benefit from our world-class, industry leading, **REVOLUTIONARY** platform. If you'd like to know more about our solution, which can save you $$$$$, then just click on the link below to request more information.

I want to learn more.

Thank you,

Customer Service
ACME AI Coding LLC

Hi Ed,

I hope all is well with you.

I read with interest your recent LinkedIn blog on AI Coding. Such an interesting piece.

Based on the points you raise in your amazing article (which we pasted to our conference room wall), we think you'll love what we are doing at ACME AI Coding.

Let me know if a brief discussion would be enjoyable for you.

Thanks,
Allison Fields, Technical Staff–ACME
afields@acme-ai-coding.ai

PS: I am an NYU Graduate!

Figure 9.1 Two different sales emails—which would you respond to?

CASE STUDY: WORLD 50

Several years ago, I was approached by the wonderful staff of World 50, an organization that provides services to executives across various sectors and disciplines. I had just retired from AT&T and was embarking on my new career as a research adviser and academic.

The staff at World 50 asked whether I would be willing to assist in setting up a new group, one that would focus on supporting senior security executives in companies. I was delighted to help, and soon after, the now successful Security 50 group emerged. The executive in charge at the time was Mike Stango (he now works in venture capital), and I can tell you that he led a master class in personalized communications.

Not only did the Security 50 team engage in tailored interactions with their members, but every so often, perhaps two or three times a year, a wrapped package would arrive (they still do) at each member's home door. Inside would be a lovely business book of interest, along with a handwritten, personalized note to the member expressing thanks for their participation and the hope that the book would be helpful and enjoyable.

This is customer service at its best, and it exemplified the power of a handwritten note. In an era of throwaway emails and spam, nothing could possibly stand out more than a company taking the time to handwrite a note to its customers.

I strongly recommend that you do something similar. It doesn't have to be a package, but a handwritten note to your customers, prospects, and leads will get noticed.

MANAGE REALISTIC SALES CYCLES

A topic I often ask start-up clients about is their sales cycle, and I usually couch the discussion with my view that there really isn't any typical sales cycle, regardless of the industry the start-up competes in. I want to understand how the sales team views their sales process from start to finish. The answers to this question often provide hints about how realistic the founding team is about its business.

The most popular answer from start-up founders is that their sales cycle is unusually short, sometimes almost negligible. "When customers see our product," I hear them say, "they buy immediately." It's tough sometimes to determine if the founders really believe this or if they offer this view to me and know that TAG is a group that speaks with buyers.

This hesitation for founders to be honest is a hazard of our business. The start-ups we coach sometimes worry that, if they expose weaknesses to our analysts, then we will pass this information along to buyers. We never expose this information (always under nondisclosure agreements [NDAs]), but it is a common fear among start-ups, and I work hard every day to fix this misconception. This book is part of that education process.

I would say that roughly 90 percent of the start-up teams we work with underestimate the length of their sales cycle. The problem is that most teams include only the buyers who have decided to buy. To do the calculation properly, however, you also need to factor in the buyers who are still on the fence and being worked.

Be careful when developing a view of your sales cycle. You really must factor in every aspect of the life cycle, from prospect research all the way to deal closure. My observation is that very few start-ups estimate a duration any less than two to three months. For complex platforms and major buyers, the time will be much, much longer. Maybe even years.

WORK ACCORDING TO A PLAN

I strongly recommend that start-up teams, and especially founders and CEOs, take time to review collectively their personal productivity and consider optimizing the most precious resource that they own—their *time*. It seems a mystery that so many founders and CEOs simply do not operate on a day-to-day basis according to a strictly planned schedule.

For example, we often see them flailing about in airport waiting areas, between meetings, traveling from here to there, attending conferences—and all without much semblance of prioritized time management. When we ask a founder how things are going, it's so much more impressive if they respond that things are being managed than the more common response that things are insane and crazy.

We often visit industry symposiums and conferences, and we inevitably hit the vendor booths. It is entertaining to see who is in the booth to meet with customers and develop leads. In most cases, the founders and CEOs will not be present in the booth. They leave this task to people who are often employees who often don't stay with the company very long.

What could these founders and CEOs possibly be doing that is a higher priority than welcoming prospects who are visiting the company's booth? I understand that this might be less reasonable for

Microsoft or Verizon, but I am talking about start-ups. In managing your time as a founder, is there really something more important than being there to welcome sales leads at your conference booth? Is your time management really that bad?

The honest reason founders might not put on the logo shirt and work the booth is because they are nervous. Perhaps worse, they might consider themselves above such mundane duty. If you work for a company where this seems to be the case, then I hope you already know my advice, which is to look for another job. Start-ups led by people who are above meeting with prospects will fail.

I once was asked to work the booth at an Armed Forces Communications and Electronics Association (AFCEA) conference for Leidos. They had hired TAG to write the security portion of a big proposal for a major bid it was working on for the Defense Information Systems Agency (DISA). The proposal was a winner, and we all enjoyed and celebrated the win. And soon after, I was asked to work the AFCEA booth.

I thought this would be fun, so I agreed to put on the Leidos logo shirt and work their booth. I might not be the most famous person around, but in government environments focused on cybersecurity, I am reasonably well known. But as the conference was set to begin, and I met the nice folks working the Leidos booth, I realized that none of them had any idea who I was, other than someone who had helped with a winning proposal. I enjoyed the relative anonymity.

Once attendees began to arrive at the booth, I really did enjoy speaking with people who wanted to learn more about our big win. But it soon became clear to the folks working the Leidos booth that something was slightly amiss. They watched as the head of AFCEA and the commander of DISA came over to pose for pictures with me and to reminisce about work we had done together while I was with AT&T.

I shared my story with the other folks from Leidos, and all was good. But here's the point: That booth was bustling with VIPs stopping to say hello. It was exhilarating to be engaged in the discussions, and I am pretty sure that I helped Leidos, my customer, establish some leads. The event was a great success, and I hope it makes my point about time management. Prioritizing one's time to select the right types of activities to cover is a great habit. That booth was the right place for me to be.

We tell founding teams and CEOs to initiate a process of double managing their time, including on workdays, worknights, weekends, and even holidays and vacations. The executive support team, if one exists, should use whatever collaboration tools are available, usually as part of Microsoft 365, to automate the management of the senior executive's calendar, and the daily plan should be visible to the entire start-up team.

We explain that a more private calendar must also be maintained and managed with all private and personal activities woven into the daily time schedule. This is important for two reasons. First, when you are running a start-up, the company becomes part of your family, almost like a new child. Its needs must be prioritized and balanced with the needs of the rest of your family and personal activities.

Second, founders should have some privacy in the tasks covered during the day, so what looks like private, blocked-off time should be managed separately and carefully reviewed by the executive. I do this personally in pencil and paper, and if you look at my daily calendar, time spent in the gym, time spent with clients, and time spent with my family are adjacent time-managed tasks, and I follow the plan, always set the night before, with religious fervor.

This process has served me well, but you should develop your own approach. Be sure that you don't fall into the trap of flailing from one thing to another with no semblance of prioritization. We view that as a trap that can destroy your company.

OUTWORK YOUR COMPETITION

I always watch to see whether a start-up management team is putting in the time. Running a start-up is not only a full-time job; it is *three* full-time jobs, and this should be true for everyone on the management team. Every successful founding team we have worked with will tell you that the time they put into their start-up was extensive and that, in retrospect, they are not sure how they ever did it.

The truth is that there needs to be a work ethic and intensity that rival the most obsessive behavior you could ever imagine, and this must be acknowledged before one ever decides to embark on a start-up. And nowhere is this more important than with the sales team. They must be a ravenous bunch whose approach to sales involves always doing things now—never later. Sales cannot wait in an early-stage start-up.

Elon Musk, for example, has moved from being a start-up founder to being essentially in his own category in many ways. He claims that he works seven days per week and takes only two or three truly workless vacation days each year. If one of the richest people on the planet has this type of work ethic, then every founding team and sales team must decide whether it will mimic this behavior.

Running a successful start-up, especially in the context of doing sales, is not a balanced, normal thing to do and will almost certainly put strains on all your relationships. This includes spouses, kids, family, and friends. We do not recommend the start-up founding lifestyle as a way to build a happy family life or even a happy life.

The start-up life is something a founding team succumbs to rather than selects. It is often described to us as an urge to achieve a vision. To accomplish this vision, founders must accept hardships that are not unlike those necessary to reach the summit of a large mountain. This means putting in the time doing work that is not always enjoyable. It means getting up at five a.m. or earlier to work sales leads.

You either put in the time or you do not. I always advise founders to share the following statement with their entire team: "There are a thousand things that start-up teams cannot control, but one thing they can control is to outwork everyone else." That's something that can be put on the company T-shirt or taped to the refrigerator in the breakroom. Hard work is one of the key aspects of start-up sales.

That observation should become the rallying cry for the entire team, and it is powerful indeed because it removes the uncertainty from at least one element of running a start-up. You do not need permission to outwork everyone else. You do not need customers, and you do not even need funding to outwork everyone else. All you need is the willingness and the strength to do so.

Which brings me to one additional side point: Every start-up founder we know that has been successful in reaching the chasm tells us that they work out regularly. Some of them run, some of them do yoga, and many hit the gym in one way or another. (I work out every morning.) This habit seems to continue as the company grows and is also true for the leaders of larger organizations. It's an interesting point to ponder, especially if you are plopped down on a chair in front of your computer right now eating a doughnut.

LEARN TO WRITE SUCCINCTLY

Think about all the unclear agendas for meetings, sloppily written brochures, overly long emails, complex legal contracts, and other bad pieces of writing that you and I are subjected to each day in the context of our sales work. AI tools like ChatGPT might make certain aspects better, but even that tool can be wordy, with GenAI sentences that start like this: "In the realm of the modern digital landscape . . ."

The truth is that most business writing between buyers and sellers is wordy and too long. Our inboxes are full of emails with multiple PDF attachments with product descriptions, data sheets, articles from content teams, and so on. The approach that weak sales teams take is that if a fifty-word email with two attachments seems good, then a one-hundred-word email with four attachments must be twice as good.

I think their arithmetic is backward. One personal skill that can help a sales team improve its numbers involves learning the art of writing. And the essence of that art is that less is more.

All business writing, especially emails to prospects, customers, and investors, should be approached as a deliberate process of developing something crisp, on point, and succinct. All emails should be drafted, reviewed, pruned, edited, and then finally sent out only when it is determined—either by the writer or some writing partner—that no extra words exist and that every word included is absolutely necessary.

We often recommend using the rule of fifty, that is, the best emails are less than fifty words. Although this is limiting, try to be succinct and ask your team to do the same. Long, rambling emails written in a stream-of-conscious manner can do considerable harm to the reputation of the writer, and they can damage a relationship with a buyer. You do not want them to cringe when they see something in their inbox from you.

Never write and send an email that is harsh, critical, or otherwise negative. Here's an example: I once bought a product from an early technologist in cybersecurity, and I will not use his name here out of respect. He was an early firewall creator, and I was a customer of one of his start-up companies.

For some reason, however, he had some private email correspondence within his company that was critical of me personally. It questioned my technical competence. Coming from him, I suspect that what he was writing was probably true. If this person thought that I didn't understand the interaction of his product with the operating system or whatever it was that he said I could not follow, then he was probably right.

What happened, unfortunately, was that someone on his team accidentally responded and copied someone on my own team, and it was eventually forwarded to me. The criticism was probably valid, but at the time, it stung. And I am ashamed to admit that I canceled our contract and never did business with that company again. I was acting exactly how most human beings act when they are criticized. I wish I had been more mature, but I wasn't.

Harsh emails have this way of sticking around and coming back to bite you later. So learn to write friendly, succinct emails. Perhaps a good idea to keep in mind is to compose emails and other notes that can be printed and taped to your recipient's refrigerator without anyone on the planet feeling bad. Avoid the harsh commentary.

The first version of this book was composed with long rambling paragraphs with wordy explanations of each point, and this approach was sufficient to obtain a book deal with Columbia University Press. But once the contract was signed, my rewrite process involved pruning every paragraph to no more than five sentences, and most are exactly that length. It is an approach that forces me to be succinct.

STOP TALKING AND LISTEN

I often run bootcamp sales sessions for our vendor customers. I've done them on weekends for literally sixteen hours, and I have also done one-hour versions. They are chock full of ideas, suggestions, hints, stories, and other points that we hope will stick with attendees. The weekend sessions are a good way to see who is willing to put in the time. Most start-ups refuse to consider full days of training on Saturday and Sunday.

Suppose that Team A has excellent and talented sales staff who spend their weekends with their family, perhaps coaching soccer, assisting with parents, or enjoying time on the golf course with friends. These are wonderful and admirable ways to unwind and spend one's free time. Good for them.

In contrast, their competition at Team B spends their weekends developing sales leads, learning about their product, and taking courses on leadership. I know these are not family friendly activities, but if you had to guess which team would drive to a more successful exit, wouldn't you choose Team B?

One exercise I use in our sales bootcamp sessions involves showing pictures of people interacting and communicating in a business setting. These can be mundane pictures from an image library, or they can be actual pictures of people chatting with someone famous such as Albert Einstein. When I select the pictures, I try to pick ones that involve one person obviously talking and the other person obviously listening.

I then ask participants during these training sessions to look at each picture and imagine that a sale is going on as part of the interaction. I ask them to dream up a scenario in which the salesperson is the one doing the talking and another scenario in which the salesperson is the one doing the listening. The results of this exercise are quite revealing and sometimes downright amazing.

In almost all cases, the start-up sales teams or other leaders in the sessions acknowledge that the stereotypical answer for each pictured scenario is for the salesperson to be the one doing the talking. The salesperson is giving the pitch.

But with the same level of uniformity, start-up sales teams agree that it would be so much better for the salesperson in the picture to be the one doing the listening. Each person agrees that when the buyer is talking, that usually signals a sale. They report that it's like a transformation, when their mind shifts in viewing the picture from the person talking and doing the selling to the person talking and doing the buying.

What does this mean in terms of start-up sales behavior? It should be obvious that you should stop talking and listen to your customer. Get them talking and show interest in what they are saying. If you are selling to them, then you must have some common interests, so demonstrate this by being attentive, supportive, and complimentary of what they are saying.

When I was in my mid-teens, I was an annoying know-it-all about literally everything, especially when I was sure that I knew better, which happened often. My dad noticed this problem, and wisely handed me a copy of a book that honestly changed my life forever: Dale Carnegie's *How to Win Friends and Influence People*.

When I read the book, I could hardly believe how many of the principles of human behavior I was violating every day with my family, friends, and others in my orbit. Since then, I have read that book fifty times or more. I must have much of it memorized, and if you are also a Carnegie disciple, then you will be "hearty in your approbation" of my own use of the book (an inside joke for people who've read and absorbed the book).

The basic thesis of the book is that human beings are fundamentally more interested in themselves than anything else on the planet. Carnegie points out that most people would be more concerned with a hangnail on their finger than they would be about a news report of many people suffering in some remote part of the world. This is powerful insight, and start-up sales teams should take note.

For example, you cannot underscore the power of helping a prospect's children. This might seem silly, but the kind act of helping the child of a colleague can be one of the most rewarding experiences. I know this can be controversial, perhaps even disallowed in some settings, so please consult your lawyer or human resources representative before you follow the raw advice that I am about to offer.

If you can extend a helping hand to the child of an associate, you will do much to cement the relationship, especially if the help you extend is sincere and done honestly. Helping them with career counseling or assisting as they review colleges where you have a connection are good examples. These are kind acts, and you'll love doing this. But they also have clear business value.

I am a professor at New York University (NYU), a position I've held since 2016. I cannot tell you how many of my business prospects have asked if I would help their high school child whose dream is to attend NYU, which only accepts 13 percent of applicants. What I always do is ask to speak privately with the young person, usually on a Zoom session. I'll offer sincere and honest feedback to this NYU prospect and then I'll dash off an honest note to admissions explaining my interaction.

This does not always work to get the youngster into the school, and I am always honest in my assessment. But it is always appreciated, and I like doing it. I hope NYU does not change its policy of allowing such interactions. Helping other people and their families is one of the more enjoyable aspects of doing sales. It sure beats sending out email solicitations.

PREPARE CONTRACT PAPERWORK IN ADVANCE

I remember a business meeting in the mid-2010s where a vendor was seated in my conference room showing my team a new information technology (IT) security tool that they had developed. I loved the concept and expressed my interest in buying. At the time, I had sufficient seniority under the local schedule of authorization to have approved the deal on the spot with my signature. And I would have signed on the spot had I been asked by the sales team.

That meeting was on a Friday morning, and the sales team agreed to get me a contract by Monday. As you would expect, I received a budget freeze notification over the weekend, and the deal was never done. Fill in the blanks on this one: Had that team developed, signed, and presented paperwork to me during the Friday meeting, they would have had a deal. The budget freeze that explicitly set aside any signed deals happened afterward.

When I obtained my first contract for TAG, I had the document printed, signed, and ready to go before I even began the negotiation. That deal would never have been done had I not prepared in advance. I came to that meeting ready to succeed. I was not prepared for failure; I was prepared for a successful signed contract. And that is what I got.

Every start-up sales team must prepare for victory in advance of every sales interaction with a potential paying customer. They must take the time to prepare nondisclosure agreements (NDAs), proof-of-concept (POC) agreements, sales agreements, or whatever paperwork is required after a customer says yes. Do not wait for them to give feedback before you prepare this material; do it in advance.

If a consumer wants to sign up for your business-to-consumer (B2C) service, then make sure they can do this on the spot with a minimum of effort. For B2B sales, always try to execute an NDA if you can. This shows that you are a serious vendor who takes the confidentiality of a business relationship seriously. Your customer will admire this, and it gets the paperwork flowing in the right direction, without requiring that your customer agree to any real purchase.

Yes, you will meet the administrative person or team that handles sales contracts, and you can use the NDA process to start developing the relationship with them. Note that if you are a new vendor, you will have to be approved by the customer's procurement process, and getting to know the right people that handle this process is so important. I've found that starting with NDAs can reduce overall sales life cycle times significantly. Try it.

A FINAL POINT ON START-UP SELLING: COMMIT

This last topic is something I cannot really coach but that must instead emerge from the start-up leadership and sales teams themselves. The issue is whether each individual on the start-up team is willing to commit to their work or not. By "commit," we mean deciding that they will do this work and that the sale of this product or service is what they were born to spend their life doing.

Customers know the difference between someone dabbling in an area versus someone truly committed to that area. This cannot be coached, but if you are a salesperson in a category such as agricultural technology, then you are likely to be competing with salespeople who might be third- or fourth-generation farmers and for whom agriculture has been a way of life for their entire existence.

In this circumstance, you might believe that your position is just a job, something you'd just as soon quit if something better came along, but your competition is telling prospects that they grew up on a farm and that they hope their kids do the same. This is why we say that start-up sales teams must truly commit to be successful.

PART FOUR

REVIEW AND PLANNING

10

WHAT IS WORKING IN YOUR START-UP?

The title of this chapter represents such a simple and straightforward question, and yet it is one that many start-up founders and CEOs generally cannot answer. The inverse question is also of interest: What is not working in your start-up? This is an even more difficult issue for start-up leaders to address, especially if they pride themselves on an aggressive can-do atmosphere of success.

A common situation we encounter when a founding team agrees to explain their progress is that they are overly optimistic about everything: things are just great, business is strong, revenue is growing, and so on. Our view is that this is usually not accurate. Perhaps you have already heard the following familiar business quip: Start-up founding teams should be short-term pessimists but long-term optimists.

This implies that the leaders of a start-up should take seriously every little thing, from competitive threats to trouble with a client, to a slight sales trend downward, and so on. These short-term issues, which might be small yellow flags to any normal person, should be bright red flags to a start-up CEO. They should be treated as stop-the-press problems, however minor they might seem, if only to ensure that they do not grow into larger and more systemic issues.

Remember that start-ups might be on a long-term mission to change the world, but they cannot do so unless they make payroll each month. Being a short-term pessimist while also being a long-term optimist is a good mindset for someone running a start-up.

What start-ups in both business-to-business (B2B) and business-to-consumer (B2C) contexts usually offer when asked what is working in their business involves factoids. We almost always hear anecdotes about a recent sale, some new feature, a great meeting with a prospect, or such and such great article that was written by an analyst.

These factoids are great for progress illustration but terrible for progress measurement. Solid metrics based on data should always serve as the basis for determining what's working and what is not. For example, if a start-up has twenty customers at the beginning of the year and adds four new trial customers during the first quarter but does not obtain renewals from four existing customers, then the chosen factoid will almost always be that the company added four new logos during the quarter.

We are treated to these types of often-misleading factoids during coaching and advisory sessions, when we are under non-disclosure and are specifically hired to understand what is actually going on. For this reason, we have concluded that too many start-up teams put themselves into a state of overly positive thinking, always emphasizing the wins and never worrying much about the losses.

The goal should be clarity, bordering on obsessive concern for every little thing in the near term combined with bold optimism about the future. In the example above, the start-up with the twenty customers should explain, when asked, that the quarter was basically flat and that a team was dispatched to understand why four customers did not renew, how to make certain that four new proofs of concept (POCs) will go well, and so on. That is a much more accurate view.

UNDERSTANDING METRICS

Every start-up founding team will readily agree that metrics are important. They are asked about metrics during their funding process where venture capital teams make their interest known regarding which types of metrics are viewed as mandatory. These include the usual types of ratios of this to that, growth rates for this or that, comparisons of volumes of one thing to another, and so on. Usually these find their way onto a dashboard, and the CEO is expected to explain the numbers on a regular basis.

It might be helpful here to provide some foundational understanding of what is really meant by "metrics." It is obviously a term that is thrown around often—and one we will repeat throughout this chapter. But if I asked you to define what is meant by "metrics," you would probably respond with something along the lines of it being a set of goals, measurements, or something like that. Let's provide an accurate grounding for you.

You should know the name Claude Shannon. He was our patron saint at Bell Labs. When I would walk into my office in Florham Park, New Jersey, I'd pass his statue in the lobby (and would often tap it for good luck). Shannon explained that a great definition of information was that it reduced uncertainty. A sender would provide information to reduce uncertainty in a receiver. An entire theory of information entropy followed, but this is a great definition.

Let's start with the premise that when a start-up is asked to provide information, it is being asked to reduce the uncertainty the requester might have about the company. The process of measurement involves connecting some quantification with information, usually in the context of a known quantity. Measurement allows you to compare some observed information with a scale that might be ordered or associated with intervals, ratios, or other factors.

A metric can be thought of as an overall system in which measurements are reviewed, compared, and connected with some defined goal. Metrics are used to measure progress and are less connected to units and numbers and more with measurements, and much more connected with the interpretation of what each of the underlying measurements actually mean. This is key because it highlights the overall purpose of any metric, which is tracking progress.

DETERMINING MARKET TIMING

The first focus area for both measurement and metrics associated with a start-up is time. Metrics almost always include the dimension of time, generally measured in units of days, weeks, and months (hours and years apply less often). Time is the most in-your-face dimension of any metric, especially because the essence of a start-up is to go faster than the competition.

The Holy Grail, obviously, is to create a metric that shows how your product or service is converging over a well-defined time period toward the perfect confluence of market need and solution availability. This is the elusive market-timing issue, and the problem is that too many founding teams and investors (customers seem savvier) believe that it is possible to predict the date where a given product/market fit is perfect, as illustrated in figure 10.1.

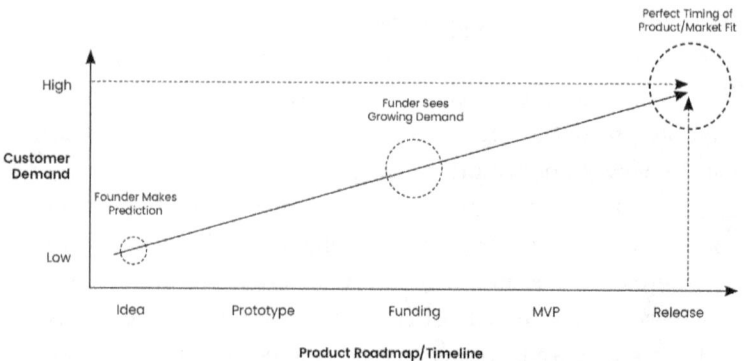

Figure 10.1 Every start-up's dream graph for product/market fit

Market timing in the context of establishing proper product/market fit is a topic that deserves additional attention, particularly in the context of determining what is working or not working in a business. The sad truth is that things are often not working because the market timing for the product being offered is just wrong. This might be avoidable, but often it is not.

A famous example is the introduction in 2000 by Microsoft of the tablet PC. Bill Gates himself unveiled the product, which had colorized screens, ran a popular operating system, and looked like it should have been a winner. Of course, we all know that it was not. Ten years later, however, Steve Jobs unveiled a similar product called the iPad that was spectacularly successful, and I believe the main reason was simple: timing.

For example, by 2010, wireless network infrastructure had progressed to 3G, which was well suited to tablet usage and allowed untethering from Wi-Fi. Also by 2010, the consumer and business markets had become used to the idea of having a smartphone with a flat, sleek-looking touch screen. The iPhone had emerged in 2008, and this provided exactly the type of training necessary for buyers to want a bigger version, namely, a tablet. The timing was perfect, which was good news for Jobs, bad news for Gates.

S-CURVES

Start-ups should study, learn, and apply the familiar S-curve model because it has served predictors of market trends reasonably well for many decades. The S-curve shape, where you pull the top tip of the S to the right a bit and then pull the bottom tip of the S to the left a bit, leaving the S-curve slightly bent and leaning to the right, matches the birth, adolescence, growth, productive years, and leveling off for a business.

As you would expect, the growth of a market, company, or other structure modeled with an S-curve begins at the bottom left. As things begin to grow, you move from left to right up the S-curve.

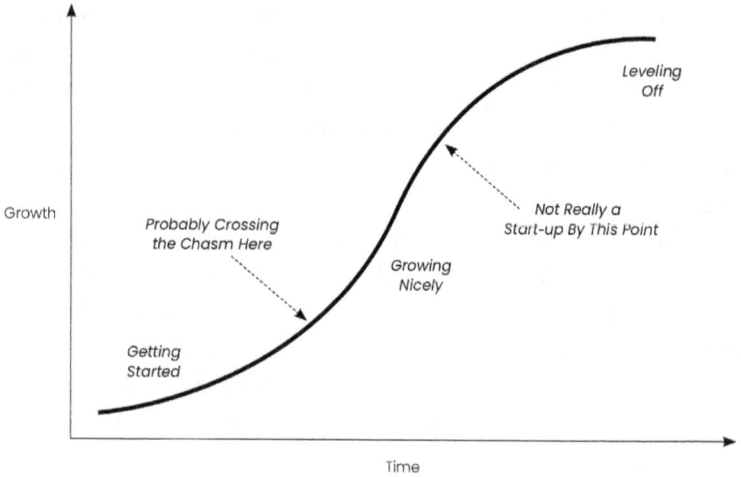

Figure 10.2 S-curve model for start-ups

The S-curve eventually levels off, however, and you move horizontally (or downward) at the top of the model. This is an accurate reflection of how things progress along a life cycle, but it is not always easy to determine where on the S-curve a given company might be (as illustrated in figure 10.2).

It is extra hard to make such a determination if a start-up or other business has several products and services that are following different progressions. The relative heights of different S-curves will vary, reflecting the sizes of markets or businesses, and the time it takes to move along the S-curve will be different, reflecting the length of time for maturity to drive from the bottom left portion of the model to the top right.

Obvious examples of S-curves from everyday business include, for instance, the wireline network infrastructure in the United States. You could model the traditional provision of wired phone service using circuit-switching technology as a long, drawn-out

S-curve beginning at the start of the twentieth century, growing through the 1930 through the 1970s, and then beginning to level off as that same century ended.

Today, that business, which accounted for the livelihood of millions of people, hardly exists. Not only has the S-curve flattened, but it has slumped off to the right. This gives a nice hint to start-ups who choose to slay the dragon. That is, when they find a traditional company that has reached the top of the S-curve, that company becomes an excellent target for business disruption.

The good news for telecommunications companies is that just as wireline services began to slow, a new S-curve emerged with wireless communications. The lower left portion of the S-curve for wireless began arguably around the 1980s and 1990s and is now in the growth and productive stages of existence, throwing off large portions of free cash flow and providing a base for businesses such as Uber and Tesla.

At some point, the best businesses will find their way to the top portion of the S-curve and level off, but it is hard to determine exactly when this occurs. This is the challenge of determining market timing, especially for start-ups. Things always look so clear after the fact, but not nearly so clear during the life cycle. Good start-ups map their solutions and those of their competitors to S-curves.

CASE STUDY: ARBOR NETWORKS

To illustrate the process of getting the market timing right, let's review a start-up called Arbor Networks, now part of NETSCOUT. Members of the TAG analyst team worked closely with this start-up for many years prior to their acquisition. We are always so proud when start-ups we coach are acquired, and I will admit to having a soft spot for Arbor Networks, an innovative company that I'd also known as a customer when I was in telecommunications.

Arbor Networks was one of the early pioneers in something called distributed denial of service (DDOS) protection. They offered a special type of internet firewall that could be used to look for incoming traffic to a website, usually from a nasty botnet of infected computers, and to provide a means for finding the bad stuff, which is dropped, and also the good stuff, which is passed through to the website.

Until about the mid-2000s, most companies used a product from Cisco Systems to perform DDOS security, but Cisco decided around that time that the product had no future, and they discontinued it in 2008. Their advice was to switch to Arbor Networks, a start-up that Cisco had apparently invested in. I remember getting the letter of product discontinuance from Cisco.

My team was soon being transitioned to Arbor Networks, a company that I frankly knew very little about. That all changed, as you would expect, and the timing for Arbor Networks was perfect because DDOS attacks began to rise. In 2012, there was a massive attack from Iran on U.S. banks, and the one device that kept these sites running was the Arbor Networks platform.

I remember speaking with many important people in Washington, DC, explaining that the websites of dozens of U.S. banks were being kept up by this little unknown start-up. Arbor Networks hit their stride just as DDOS attacks were rising up the S-curve, from a few megabits per second (just a drop to a network engineer) to a few terabits per second today (which is enough to get a network engineer's attention for sure).

TEAM COMPOSITION

Another important factor on whether things are working or not working in your company is your mix of people. By this, I don't mean just the management team but the entire team. It's tough unfortunately to develop a metric to measure the quality of your team composition other than perhaps average number of years of experience, number of advanced degrees, and so on. These are not useful metrics, in my view.

We have found instead that start-ups benefit by following one of several well-known models for setting up team composition. The first involves a group of people who previously worked together at another firm. This can work well if the chemistry is right, but be careful not to create a subteam within your team. At TAG, we have quite a few former AT&T folks, so we always have to be mindful to include others when we reminisce.

Another common model involves hiring a group of people from a common tribe. A start-up might, for example, hire only research scientists with biochemistry degrees. This helps to establish a team composition that is science-based and probably pretty technical in their discussions. Initial customers presumably would be attracted to this culture and would feel strongly connected to the culture.

There is also the famous founder and team of disciples model that establishes more of a top-down team composition. I often listen, for example, to the podcast of Scott Galloway, a fellow New York University (NYU) faculty member. His current company includes a wonderful staff of young people who are set up to support, promote, and complement Galloway. A diagram of their company would look like a pyramid, with Galloway at the top.

Of course, there is also the serial founder model, which involves a successful founder who has exited previously and, after some time, conjures up a start-up with venture capital investors who put together a company based on people they select from their network and place into designated positions. Note that buyers do not always take well to your comments about that yellow Ferrari and small island you own. So be careful with this one.

The bottom-line regarding team composition is not the specific model you choose but that you choose one and celebrate its effectiveness for your purposes. Buyers will watch carefully to see that you have a coherent story. Pay close attention to how you put your team together.

HIRE SLOWLY, FIRE QUICKLY

One metric often missed when reviewing the effectiveness of a start-up is the time it takes to hire and fire staff. I am always amazed when a founding team bragged about how quickly they have added a large number of staff in a short period of time. I view such speed-to-hire as a massive negative.

I have learned through experience that every start-up should follow this golden rule when it comes to hiring and firing: Start-ups should hire slowly but fire quickly. That is one to write down and memorize. It is one of the more important statements we have made in this book.

When a manager decides to add staff in a large company like IBM or Verizon, they are making a decision that affects roughly one-two-hundred-thousandth of the entire staff culture. They want to get this right, but if they get it wrong, the impact is marginal at best to the firm. One bad hire to a company such as Bank of America is not going to affect the success of the firm, unless we are talking about the CEO or other major executive, of course.

But when an early-stage start-up decides to add someone to their team, they might be making a decision that affects roughly one twentieth or thirtieth of the entire staff culture. A large company might do some interviews, background checks, and reference discussions in advance of hiring a new staff, but start-ups should do so much more simply because so much more is at stake.

At TAG, we believe we have taken this process to an art form. When we hire new staff, we typically ask them to work for a period of time as a part-time member of the team making next-to-nothing as salary. If they balk at our offer, then we are probably talking to the wrong person. We work for purpose, and we seek those who share the same goal. But if they seem excited and say that they really want to do the work with us, then we bring them in and start to evaluate.

But when it comes to firing, things should not be drawn out. When the CEO or other founding executive gets that feeling that someone just does not fit, then the company would probably be stronger without that person in the mix. When that feeling arises, action should be taken immediately, now.

This can be a terrible situation, especially if you have hired colleagues, family members, or friends. But you must be resolute: If you think the company is better off without some individual, then you simply have to act, even if that person might have been there from the beginning. And by "act," I mean "fire." You cannot second-guess yourself, and you cannot hesitate because you will lose your company if you do.

This can be tricky because that feeling is sometimes not always so obvious. You might be wavering between keeping the person and firing them. Our advice to start-ups is that if you are wavering, then fire the person in question. Working for a start-up is a brutal gamble, one that every employee should understand is like walking a tight rope blindfolded. If someone wants low risk and career stability, and neither can be promised by any employer, then perhaps they should work for a bigger company.

I can tell you that we have never once heard of a start-up saying that they fired someone too fast. It is always the opposite: that they fired too slowly. This is a problem because B and C performers can easily infect A players down to the lower levels. You must act quickly, even if the person involved is a friend. If you value the friendship more than your company, then you cannot be a start-up founder.

MEASURING PROGRESS

If you have venture capital or private equity investors, then they will weigh in on how they expect you to report progress. You have to conform to their reporting wishes because you did agree to take their money. They will protect their investment by demanding that you report your progress on a dashboard, and the ultimate unit of progress will be the rate of closed deals, that is, sales.

Regardless of your funding situation, leadership teams must perform the difficult but essential task—more art than science—of determining what should be measured and against what set of metrics such measurements should be evaluated. For example, everyone measures sales results, but only a leadership team can determine which factors are important guideposts to measure toward successful outcomes.

Suppose the data reveal that, for every fifty prospect leads, you connect reliably with ten of them. The data further suggest that for every ten connections you make, you get five meetings, which result collectively in one signed deal. If this is your math, then you know that, for every fifty leads, you're probably going to get one signed deal. That is a reasonable metric that can be tracked each month.

One problem we see is that, because start-ups change staff frequently, it is not unusual for the metrics, reporting, and other measures of progress to shift with these changes of staff. Our guidance is that founding teams should establish a baseline. It is reasonable to allow new start-up team members to propose metrics they are comfortable with, but too much change will make it tough to spot meaningful trends over the long term.

CASE STUDY: OBJECTIVES AND KEY RESULTS (OKR) FRAMEWORK

A metrics approach that I see referenced is called objectives and key results (OKR). This methodology was created by Intel's former CEO Andy Grove in the 1970s and was popularized for start-ups by venture capital investor John Doerr. The general approach in OKR is that ambitious objectives are set by an organization and then progress is measured in achieving such goals through a series of incremental subgoals.

The OKR framework has two parts: First, the organization defines clear aspirational statements of what it hopes to achieve. These statements tend to work best when they are specific and associated with owners and completion dates. Vague goals such as "Sell more subscriptions" are not helpful as aspirational statements. They have to express a specific goal, such as "We must sell ten new units by October to our top forty clients."

Second, the organization creates metrics that define interim goals, and again, these metrics are best with target dates that provide a road map to establishing the objective. This might involve establishing a set number of prospects to be contacted by a certain date. An expected number of responders would then be contacted for a sales discussion within some number of days. These discussions would then result in some designated number of proposals being written by a set date.

Doerr emerged as the most famous supporter of the OKR message; he wrote a book called *Measure What Matters*, which makes the case for the approach. He claims to have mentored the Google founders on OKR, and much has been made of how the framework scaled nicely as the search company grew. It seems like nothing bad can come from a start-up adopting OKR or something similar.

My view is that the specific goal-setting framework selected really doesn't seem to matter as long as something is in place. OKR has the advantage of having many present and former adopters as well as many pages of material explaining how it works. If you search online, you will find excellent guidance on OKR and how it's apparently viewed as just about the greatest thing since sliced bread to its devotees.

If you decide to use it, then stick with it and try to include tough stretch goals in your plan. Not everything you do should be a simple layup. Some business advisers refer to these stretch goals as big hairy audacious goals (BHAGs). Apart from the gross visual image that BHAGs create, they do reinforce the idea that companies, and especially start-ups, should be pushing themselves hard.

DEALING WITH INVESTOR BOARDS

When you accept funding from venture capital, you will no doubt have to deal with a somewhat formal board, which, for convenience, we will refer to as an "investor board." The real investors, sometimes including rich individuals and family trust funds, might be less visible to the start-up, having provided their cash to the venture capital team for investment. The board represents the interests of these investors. One side-goal you should consider as founder is to make sure that you are okay, perhaps morally, with the groups giving money. You can learn about these groups during your early discussions with venture capital groups.

This goal of representing the investors is important for start-up teams to understand when they are dealing with an investor board. Investors usually have not given money to a venture capital team because they believe in the vision of some start-up; they value a relationship with a start-up; or they love the great benefit that will accrue to customers, perhaps including country or military users.

Investment teams represented by investor boards of venture capitalists have given money to the start-up because they expect a positive financial return—and they want a great aggregate financial return across all their investments. Your start-up will probably be just one pea in their much bigger pod of financial bets. That is what you are to venture capital: a financial bet. Get over any feelings of love for your venture capitalists. You can respect them but don't love them.

What this implies is that this board will be listening through a financial framework. They are there for money, that is their right.

You should know that if an investor board views it in their best interests to break up your start-up and sell the parts, then they will do so. While contract management, term sheets, and the specifics of a venture capital deal are well beyond the scope of this book, I will say that it is laughable when a start-up team explains to us that, because they control over 51 percent of the company stock, the venture capital team has no power. This is not how it works.

When you bring venture capital into the picture, regardless of the financial split, you have handed them the steering wheel. Any reporting you provide regarding progress will be translated into units of dollars by every attendee in an investor board meeting. You will benefit by knowing that this is occurring, and we always coach start-up teams to be aware of this phenomenon.

What is the best way to deal with such financial pressure? Make your numbers. Meet the goals you established. Show that you are making progress according to a plan. These are not easy goals, but this is how you tame an investor board. There really is no other way.

CREATING ADVISORY BOARDS

Advisory boards are much different than investor boards. They are about as different as a teenager might view their parents from their friends. When you select an advisory board, you have one of three options. You could probably do all three, but it would seem an inordinate amount of work. You would be wise to review the options below and decide which suits your team best.

First, there is the advisory board that is comprised of several big personalities with big names and big reputations in your industry. This approach establishes that you know people and that if someone should dare to question your expertise, then they can go ask this or that famous person on the advisory board. If you take this approach, you run the risk of buyers seeing this as a vanity play. It is not my favorite option, to be honest.

Second is the advisory board that is customer-dominated. This type of group is established to give voice to the users of your widget and to allow them to provide a running stream of suggestions on how to improve its features. Product managers often benefit from having a customer advisory board. Our only coaching here is that you include the actual users of your product versus their supervisors.

Third is the active and engaged advisory board of experts who are encouraged and incentivized to provide real guidance and advice to your start-up. This is, in our estimation, the best type of advisory board, but there is a major issue that must be recognized. If you do this type of board, you had better convince them through your actions that you are actually listening to their recommendations.

Nothing kills a good advisory board more than going through the motions, asking for the opinions of its members, and then ignoring them, regardless of which of the three types you choose. If this is your approach, then you are better off not doing the advisory board in the first place.

11

SHOULD YOU REALLY BE DOING A START-UP?

In this final chapter, I'd like to close out our time together with a question that I ask a founder only when I feel like we have connected on a personal and trusted level. I say this because this question can produce an emotional response, at least when the founder is really being honest and introspective.

The question is this: Should you really be doing a start-up? This is not a business question, but a personal one.

There's a joke in the United States that people on the West Coast make things so that people on the East Coast can sell them. The joke is intended to highlight two mindsets. One is around disruption, innovation, and change to the status quo, whereas the other is around marketing, selling, and distribution. The joke would seem to imply that maybe Stanford University in California is a better start-up incubator than, say, New York University, but that New York might be the better option for learning the art of selling. It can be fun, I guess, to play with such stereotypes.

As I have learned, however, both mindsets are necessary. This is not something that is easily covered by one founder or by a small founding team. But I have learned—and this is another point to ponder carefully as you look in the mirror—that you must try. I would say that the most successful founders I have encountered in my decades of experience tend to possess both mindsets: They are disrupters, but they are also sellers.

Ask yourself as a founder: Do I have both mindsets? If you do not, then your odds of success drop, not to zero, of course, but you will struggle. You can build a founding team that will addresses your deficiencies, perhaps with technical founders luring in an accountant to the founding team, or with marketer founders attracting a developer to the founding team. I understand the playbook. But both mindsets need to be in place for each and every founder.

Despite the challenge, everyone on a start-up founding team should possess skills at both making things and selling them. Both mindsets must be present across leadership. I know this is somewhat inconsistent with guidance you might have received previously, where it is considered fine for one founder to be the money person, their partner founder to be the product person, and so on.

But I believe this to be a disadvantage. If you are doing a start-up, whether as a single founder or a group, there should be a confluence of capabilities among all principals in both the development of solutions and their sales.

ENTREPRENEUR VERSUS EXECUTIVE

My supervisor for many years at Bell Labs, Hossein Eslambolchi, understood the distinction between entrepreneurs and executives. Despite having hundreds of patents himself, Eslambolchi was adept at managing large teams in large organizations. He knew what it took to run a large, established group, and this did not include entrepreneurial tendencies.

That person is trying to be an entrepreneur, he would point out to us sometimes. And despite his personal experience as an inventor, his comment was not intended as a compliment in a large company.

Big companies generally do not need entrepreneurs; they need individuals who can follow plans and execute. This is a different albeit valuable skill. Executives do not nimbly drive a start-up toward the chasm and eventually over it. Executives have a much different mindset, one that combines execution with stewardship and, perhaps above all else, an intense focus on risk management. Large companies have much to lose. Start-ups have much less to lose.

If we view the executive versus entrepreneur issue in the context of an S-curve (see figure 11.1), then we can see that within a growing company, there will be evolving needs for the business leaders. At the lower portions of the S-curve, during the period of trying to reach the chasm, entrepreneurs are needed who possess that combined mindset to create and sell, whereas at the higher levels, executive skills focused on organization and risk management become vital.

When I was an executive at AT&T, I could walk into any external conference, public meeting, or industry gathering, and everyone in the room knew my company. During my long tenure, I met with presidents, senators, and major business leaders, and they were respectful. Of course, it was AT&T, not me, they were respecting. They were illustrating their admiration for a firm that had been in business for over a century. I was just there as the representative.

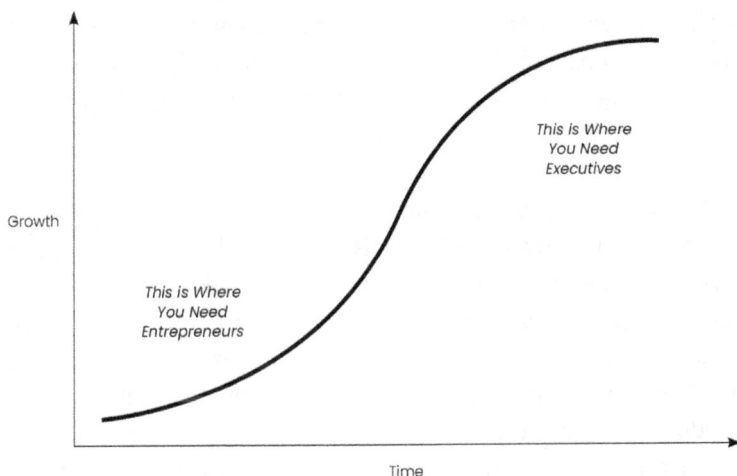

Figure 11.1 Mapping entrepreneurs and executives on the S-curve

But now that I run a start-up, I have to work hard to earn that respect. "TAG who?" is a reaction that I hear all too often, followed by, "Never heard of your company." I so desperately want to point out that I was once a big important executive and that I helped run one of the largest companies in the world. I don't do this, of course, because I understand that recognition and respect do not come hot off the presses with a start-up. You have to earn both.

To work in a start-up, you have to be prepared for zero recognition of you or your company. Nothing will come to you for free. When customers are coming for a demonstration, you will not only give the briefing, but you will also run over to the nearest coffee shop to order coffee in advance. This must be a situation you can accept, or the start-up route is just not for you. If you want immediate respect, then get a job with McKinsey or IBM.

WHAT ARE YOUR PERSONAL GOALS?

I spend time in Hoboken, New Jersey, on occasion with my friend Mickey Bresman, CEO of cybersecurity start-up Semperis and one of the best entrepreneurs in the business. I always ask him about his company because it seems that 100 percent of my own clients need what Semperis sells. But one time, over coffee, the conversation awkwardly pointed back toward me, and I found Bresman asking me about my own business.

No one ever does this, and I was unprepared for the question. "What are your own personal goals, Ed?" he asked. As I recall, this was in the context of whether I would ever take funding from a venture capital group. "What do you and your family really want?" he asked. "What are your personal goals?" After years of rolling my eyes at bad answers from founders in many different start-ups, I suddenly realized that I was struggling with my own question.

On my way home that night, I thought about my answer, and I realized that I am a disruptor. My personal goal is to disrupt, and the journey to disrupt is my destination. As long as I can provide for my family, I am happy when I can locate hypocrisy, identify inefficiency, or slay some large dragon. That is what makes me happy, and it is why I am better suited to the start-up world than the corporate one.

What does this mean for you? It should be obvious: Do you want to be comfortable, associated with a well-known brand, and proud to be wearing the logo? I can assure you that this is an excellent approach to work life. I did it for thirty-one years. Or would you prefer instead to grind things out at an unknown company, where you will get nothing for nothing, and you must claw your way through the mud for every little thing?

The start-up life is not a comfortable life. There is no personal driver waiting to take you to the airport. But if you feel like this crazy business of disruption and innovation matches what's in your head, then you are probably well-suited to a start-up. While I am excited for you, I am also sorry for you because your life would be so much smoother as a consultant at KPMG or a developer at Google.

WHAT ARE YOUR PERSONAL FINANCES?

We are not headhunters or recruiting specialists at TAG, but we do frequently hear from professionals, especially in technical or IT positions, who are looking for a new position. I recently received a request from someone working at a large bank in its IT department doing cybersecurity work. She felt she needed a change, perhaps working for a vendor or a nonprofit, and so I agreed to chat.

When we got into the details of her salary requirements, she happened to mention that she was making $600,000 per year and wanted to maintain at least that amount. This was apparently an absolute requirement, so naturally I recommended that she stick with her job or at least confine her search to Wall Street. No one is paying IT folks, even with security experience, that kind of money.

And here is the lesson from this story: If you and your family depend on a high salary, then the start-up route is not for you.

Start-ups are fraught with risk, and you could lose your position more quickly than at an established firm in most cases. The highest paying jobs at a start-up will be in sales, with the chances of making between $200,000 and $400,000 being somewhat typical at a tech start-up. It will be lower at other types of start-ups.

The founders and CEOs of most of the start-ups I have worked with often make less than the salespeople, perhaps in the range of $200K to $300K per year. And that range is for the most experienced start-up founders working in high-salary locations like San Jose, California, or New York City. If you are pre-revenue or bootstrapping your start-up with family money, then your salary is likely to be closer to zero—yes, zero.

You must think through your personal finances before you ever take the plunge. When I coach founders and they are willing to be more candid, I do occasionally meet talented people who are struggling with their personal finances. They often do not share this information until we are well into the relationship, but it's painful to hear when they do share, and there is little advice anyone can give.

To do a start-up properly, you need the luxury of focus. Trouble feeding the family can cloud your mind. For younger founders, we often hear them discuss their fantasy of being in a start-up that is coding furiously over days and nights and then launches the product, and they can watch as thousands and then millions flock to the website and the money begins to flow—and everyone gets rich.

It is a nice story, but then there is reality. The garage-to-riches story almost never happens. Think through your personal finances before you take the start-up plunge.

WHAT IS YOUR PERSONAL SUPPORT NETWORK?

I did not offer guidance in this book on the venture capital term sheet and contractual funding portion of the start-up process because this process demands that you hire the right people with the right expertise. There are many excellent financial advisers, lawyers, and other specialists who can guide you through the process of reviewing proposed terms from investors, venture capital teams, private equity, and even acquisition opportunities.

But here's the catch: If you do not have such people in your personal network or at least several who are connected to your personal network (someone that someone you know knows), then you probably don't have the personal business support network to do a start-up. This doesn't mean that you shouldn't chase your dream with a start-up company, but not having financial experts available to you on speed dial does place you at a disadvantage.

There is a more important question regarding support networks: Does your family support your career decision? It's not unusual for a start-up to be missing its numbers because the principals are distracted with uneven support or even a total lack of support from their inner circle at home. This is unfortunately more common than one would expect.

It was relatively easy for me to jump into a start-up because I had already had a long career; had shepherded my three children through their heavy tuition years; and was (and am) supported by my wife Lee, who considered the decision a good one. She took the time to train on QuickBooks and is now our full-time bookkeeper and helps with administration. She's the perfect partner for a start-up founder.

This type of support for a start-up endeavor is as valuable an asset as $10 million from an investor. If you don't have this support, then you are probably already feeling the weight of that struggle. There is no coaching I can offer other than to point out the challenge.

WHY ARE YOU DOING A START-UP?

This brings us to the end of our time together in this book, and I hope my advice, guidance, and case studies have been useful. You might have been wondering throughout this book why we spent so much time on the founder's personal situation, support networks, belief systems, and other seemingly soft concepts. My view is that these are the main drivers for meeting your numbers.

The Hollywood version of the start-up team tossing Frisbees and then reveling as their amazing invention makes them rich is just about as real as winning the lottery. It does happen, but it very likely won't happen to you. Your odds are just so such better if everything is in place, as we have discussed throughout this book. So please set this book aside, and get back to work because, if you are part of a start-up, the work never ends. Good luck.

ACKNOWLEDGMENTS

I'd like to thank our amazing start-up customers and team members at TAG Infosphere Inc., both past and present (and future). Without their amazing partnership and guidance, this book could never have been written. They have taught me what it means to drive a start-up to scale.

My academic colleagues at New York University, as well as Brian Smith, my capable editor from Columbia University Press, have all been super-supportive. I am also indebted to my many friends and colleagues at the Stevens Institute of Technology. That community has played such an important role in my career development.

During the writing of the book, Marianne L'Abbate and Ben Kolstad found ways to entertain me with some witty points while correcting my lousy choices of words, references, and perpetual forgetfulness in referencing figures. They have influenced my writing for sure. Lester Goodman was also kind enough to fix my sloppy figures.

My wife Lee and my family (Steph, Matt, Sam, and Alicia) have been so patient and understanding of the considerable amount of time that I put into my work. They have gotten used to my eyes glazing and my mind drifting off during a family discussion while I ponder some point for one of my chapters. I'll try to pay better attention now that the book is done.

INDEX

Page numbers in *italics* represent illustrations or tables.

GPSR Authorized Representative: Easy Access System Europe, Mustamäe tee
50, 10621 Tallinn, Estonia, gpsr.requests@easproject.com

www.ingramcontent.com/pod-product-compliance
Lightning Source LLC
Chambersburg PA
CBHW021459180326
41458CB00051B/6886/J